Movers, Shakers and Change Makers

Movers, Shakers and Change Makers

Royal Publishing, Inc.
P.O. Box 1120
18825 Hicrest Road
Glendora, California 91740

First Edition

Library of Congress Cataloging in Publication Data in Progress

ISBN 0-934344-21-3

Printed in the United States of America

Throughout the centuries there were those who took first steps down new roads armed with nothing but their own vision.
                              - Ayn Rand

JIM ROHN
22994 El Toro Road
El Toro, CA 92630
(714) 951-5740

Jim Rohn

Jim Rohn is one of the most sought-after business leaders today. He frequently gives seminars for top sales organizations and management groups and has been a keynote speaker for some of this country's leading conventions.

With a tremendous word-of-mouth following, Jim's tape programs alone have reached an estimated one million listeners.

His reputation as a dynamic and effective trainer and speaker has swept across America and internationally to Australia and Canada where he appears annually and to Spain, the U.K., Taiwan, New Zealand, and South Africa.

For more than twenty-five years Jim has devoted his life to the study of behavior as it affects performance. The result of this study is a profoundly simple philosophy that is sprinkled with humor yet filled with powerful down-to-earth advice to help anyone become more productive and fulfilled.

Introduction—

by Jim Rohn

All the successful Movers and Shakers with whom I have had contact are good readers. They read, read, read. It's their curiosity that drives them to read. They simply *have* to know. They constantly seek new ways to become better. Here is a good phrase to remember: ALL LEADERS ARE READERS.

There used to be a time when publishing always referred to printed matter, such as books. But today we can learn through the miracle of electronic publishing as well. I'm referring to audio tapes and videotapes, both of which are excellent ways to acquire knowledge.

Many of the busiest people I know use audio cassettes to learn during unproductive times. For example, they often listen to tapes while driving in their cars. Listening to cassettes is an easy way to pick up innovative ideas and new skills.

Did you know there are thousands of books and tapes on how to be stronger, more decisive, a better speaker, a more effective leader, a better lover; develop influence; find a mate; become more sophisticated; start a business—and thousands of other useful topics? And yet many people do not use this wealth of knowledge. How do you explain that?

Did you further know that thousands of successful people have committed their inspiring stories to paper? And yet people don't want to read. How would you explain *that?*

Our "guy" is busy, I guess. He says, "Well, yeah. But you work where I work, by the time you struggle home it's late. You've got to have a bite to eat, watch a little TV to relax, and go to bed. You can't stay up half the night and read, *read,* READ." And this is the guy who is behind on his bills. He's a good worker, a hard worker, a *sincere* worker. Hey, you can be sincere and work hard all your life and still wind up broke, confused, *and* embarrassed. You've got to be better than a good worker. You've got to be a good reader. And if you don't like to read, at least you can listen to a good cassette on the way home, right?

Now you don't have to read books or listen to tapes half the night (although if you're broke, it's not such a bad idea). All I ask is that you devote just thirty minutes a day to learning. That's all.

You want to *really* do well? Then stretch your thirty minutes to a full hour. But at least spend thirty minutes. Oh yes, here's one more thing: Don't miss. Miss a meal, but not your thirty minutes of learning. All of us can afford to miss a few meals, but none of us can afford to lose out on ideas, examples, and inspirations. Think of your reading time as "tapping the treasure of ideas" time.

Remember: YOU ARE WHAT YOU READ.

Reprinted by permission of Prima Publishing and Communications.

Find the opportunity in every situation.

— P. T. Barnum

JOHN MORLEY
758-C Calle Aragon
Laguna Hills, CA 92653
(714) 837-9574

x

John Morley

John Morley was born in Paris, France, American father, French mother; educated in Europe and United States; University of Chicago; Blackstone College of Law, Degrees LL B, J. D., LL D; Oxford University, England. He's been a Shriner and Rotarian for 45 years. United States Olympic Swimming Team qualifier. Played professional football, baseball, basketball.

He is in his 40th-year as a News-Analyst on the Platform, TV News, Radio, in the United States and abroad.

John was President Reagan's recent emissary to President Chiang Ching-Kuo, Republic of China.

From the Hitler-headlines to today's headline world, he has covered world-leaders and world-shaking events. Officially accredited War-Correspondent by the Department of Defense in the Korean and Vietnam Wars.

His syndicated column, "After Hours" circles the globe. Author of "I Believe"...now writing his latest book, "Eye-Witness To Headline History."

He is former Director of a Security of War Information campaign against foreign spies, saboteurs, terrorists... directed by the FBI, CIA, Army-Navy-Air Force Intelligence.

He has won 28 Awards for speaking and reporting. Among them, The Los Angeles Philanthropic Foundation Award: "For Outstanding News-Analysis and Staunch Support of American Ideals." Past recipients have been President Reagan, FBI Director Hoover, General Bradley, John Wayne.

Distinguished Author-News Analyst, Lowell Thomas, called him: "Marco Polo Morley...the most traveled, experienced, respected Reporter on the platform."

San Francisco Town Hall, since 1933 among the most prestigious in the nation, announced: "The three greatest speakers to appear repeatedly at Town Hall are: Sir Winston Churchill, Dr. Norman Vincent Peale, John Morley."

A Personal Note About The Publisher, Dottie Walters
By John Morley

I first met Dottie on the way up in her speaking career in Washington, D.C., in 1966. She was attending the 63rd Annual Convention of the International Platform Association, during my second term as President. Among our 7,000 members were such prominent personalities as: President Lyndon Johnson, Ronald Reagan, General Matthew Ridgeway Victor Borge, Bette Davis, Joan Crawford, Bob Considine, Drew Pearson, John Cameron Swayze, Frank Capra, Dr. Ralph Bunche and many other celebrities. President Johnson and Vice President Walter Mondale addressed the Convention.

Dottie had come all the way from California to meet and hear the platform pros. She learned fast and developed into one of the nation's outstanding speakers...and an excellent exponent of training techniques for speakers.

She authored a number of books and training manuals for speakers. She founded "Sharing Ideas," an outstanding journal for speakers and meeting planners. She conducts periodic speakers seminars, with her efficient daughter, Lilly, and "Dinners With Dottie," where prominent speakers share their expertise. With her husband, Cowboy Bob, she operates "The Royal Publishing Company." With Lilly, she runs "The Walters International Speakers Bureau." She has served on the Board of Directors of the prestigious "National Speakers Association."

Dottie has earned an international reputation as a speaker and as an excellent exponent of the art. It is this extraordinary background and achievements that have made her counsel and her books so popular among professional and amateur speakers.

Foreword—

By John Morley

News-Analyst On The Platform, TV, Radio in the U.S. and Abroad...Winner of 28 Awards for Speaking & Reporting.

Let us start at the beginning. I have never known a born-speaker, in my 40 years on the professional platform...nor as President of a prominent Speakers Association of over 7,000 professionals.

Nor have I ever heard of a born-reporter, born-doctor, lawyer, engineer, salesman, teacher or born-anything.

Generally people choose a career. And if that choice is compatible with expectations, they train, persevere and stick with it.

No matter what kind of speaker you are today...you'll be the same 5 years from today...unless...you keep your eye on the ball, by training, preparing, updating your material to meet changing conditions...and most important, by keeping close tabs on today's popular speakers and how they sustain their popularity.

I was about 8 years old when I heard my first great speaker. He moved a thousand boys with his eloquence at a Chicago YMCA Youth Rally. He was the Great Commoner, William Jennings Bryan. When he finished his speech, a rousing standing ovation greeted his upraised arms. I rushed to the platform to meet him. He smiled, bent over his tall frame and shook my hand. I summoned the courage to ask him for his advice on how to become a great speaker. (I got the bug early). He placed his hand on my head and said: "Young man, to become a good speaker, just make sure that you know more than half of your audience on what you're going to talk about." It was my first important lesson in public speaking. It sounded like our Boy Scout motto: "Be Prepared."

Good speakers thoroughly understand the importance of preparation and training. To me it remains a prophetic truism. As a matter of personal pride I try to prepare for everything important. From my youthful participation in sports, to college and professional competition. (The only thing that I recall doing without plan or preparation, was my elopement with my high school sweetheart at age 16. Since it worked, I can be forgiven.)

As a Correspondent, in 53 world newstrips to date, preparation in my case extracted a very high price. It means putting life and limb on the line in danger-zones where even my insurance does not cover me, to gather eye-witness facts. I feel the need for this kind of preparation to give me added confidence when I face a sophisticated audience and in writing my syndicated column. Eye-witness facts remain my professional trademark and my persistent goal to this day.

From the Stalin-Hitler headlines to today's headline world, I have met and heard some of the greatest speakers in the world. It's been my training ground. I witnessed world leaders change the course of their nations and of history, not always favorably, through their power of speech persuasion. I saw labor leaders here, with the gift of dynamic speech, drive workers to anarchy and violence in the early days of the labor movement. I saw religious fanatics mesmerize the masses into literal frenzy that led to murder and human convulsion, from Iran to Indonesia. My records show that the most world-shaking news-events I have covered were largely affected by powerful speakers.

Our world has not witnessed a more compelling instrument than dynamic speech. I have heard some of the best in the world who use it for good and those who pervert it for evil...A Churchill or a Hitler, Pope Pius XII or Khomeini, Sadat or Arafat, Chiang Kai-shek or Chou En-Lai, a Ben Gurion or Kadaffi, a Nehru or Castro, Magsaysay or a Marcos. Eloquent women speakers I covered included...Eleanor Roosevelt, Madame Chiang Kai-shek, Indira Gandhi, Golda Meier, Queen Frederika (Greece), Princess Grace. And more recently...Margaret Thatcher, Jeanne Kirkpatrick, Justice Sandra Day O'Connor.

My Editors would often assign me to write profiles of prominent executives, authors, theologians, who were also outstanding speakers...William F. Buckley, William Randolph Hearst, Walter Lippmann, Ernest Hemingway, H. L. Mencken, who included my writings in his popular large volume, "A New Dictionary of Quotations"; Dr. Lin Yutang, author of world famous "Importance of Living," and former President of the University of Singapore, during my lecture residency there; Reverend Billy Graham, John Patterson, President, National Cash Register; Charles M. Schwab, President, U.S. Steel and protege of Andrew Carnegie.

Training and preparation for speakers today is more important than ever, because today's audiences are more sophisticated than ever. They are better educated, better informed, better traveled...exposed to greatly improved news-coverage. They have greater access to good books, general and trade magazines, TV educational programs, training cassettes, films, news-letters, lectures. Today's growing speed of communications have shrunk our world to greater interdependence and concern, the principle of being our brother's keeper. Important news-events from around the world are flashed on our TV screens in minutes or hours. Efficient time-saving appliances and devices release more time for intellectual and educational pursuits and greater awareness of what's going on around us.

Today's more critical world events increase peoples' anxieties and the need for more dialogue with informed speakers. Like the on-going debates on dictatorships, terrorism, armament races, nuclear power, illicit drugs, sex deviation, explicit magazines, films, plays, abortion... and most important, fear of nuclear war.

There is an increasing need for speakers in the corporate community, through conventions, conferences, seminars and motivating sessions; also at universities, colleges and forums. The immediate concerns about foreign trade competition, domestic mergers, Federal budget deficits, fluctuation of the dollar, inflation, labor disputes, automation, balance of payments, taxes, jobs. All have increased the demand for dialogue by business and finance authorities.

On my national speaking tours I see a lecture-explosion in most categories. Inspirational and enter-taining speakers are in greater demand. Humorists are very popular.

The increased demand for good speakers also increases their responsibility. This is translated in better training, better preparation, better all around performance and pursuit of excellence. In this highly competitive profession, professional standards must be upgraded. This includes preparation of brochures and publicity, press releases, introduction sheets, etc.; improved public relations with the press and clients; greater focus on audience needs and preferances; appropriate personal grooming, diction and decorum on the platform.

What does it take to be a good speaker? Include the following list with others: It takes DESIRE, PREPARATION, TRAINING, CONSISTENT IMPROVEMENT, EXPERIENCE, DEDICATION, RELIABILITY, RESPONSIBILITY, OPTIMISM, SINCERITY, ACCOMMODATION, SACRIFICE, CULTIVATION OF VOICE AND LANGUAGE, DICTION, DIGNITY, DECORUM, CLEAN HUMOR, RESPECT FOR AUDIENCE... AND A FULL COMMITMENT TO EXCELLENCE.

This book you're holding, Dottie Walter's MOVERS, SHAKERS and CHANGE MAKERS, is a professional speaker's answer-book, with successful speakers providing the answers not obtainable anywhere else. Speech and speaking is updated by those who nourish it. It's an excellent pipe-line of proven methods to help you become...a better speaker. I urge you to read it, reread it, digest it and go for it. When you feel ready and have no Agent, it will help you to get one. You'll be a better speaker tomorrow, with all the rewards that go with it, for having read it today. I wish you success.

"To see things in the seed: this is Genius."

—Lao Tze

Movers, Shakers and Change Makers

CONTENTS

Movers, Shakers and
Change Makers

JOE LARSON
Sparta Brush Co.
10040 E. Happy Valley Rd.
Scottsdale, AZ 85255
(800)356-8366 (602)585-4344

Cavett
Award

Joe Larson

After thirty years of exceptional leadership, the eyes of Joe Larson, successful Sparta, Wisconsin business executive and speaker, glow with eagerness and excitement.

"Hooked on people," Joe has gained national prominence for his speaking skills. Hundreds of trade associations, civic and fraternal organizations have featured him as their keynote program, often referring to him as another "Herb Shriner." The National Speakers Association named Joe as president in 1977-78. He served as treasurer for five years. In 1983 NSA bestowed upon him the Cavett Award, "the Emmy of the Speaking World." Joe Larson views his three decades of speaking as an opportunity to motivate young people, and increase the insight of those who have already "arrived."

A Fuller Brush and Jewel Tea veteran, he acquired the slumbering Sparta Brush company in 1949. Through his enthusiasm and know-how, he nourished it into an international manufacturer of brushes for the dairy and food service industries.

He is past director of the National Assoc. of Food Equipment Manufacturers; is recipient of the distinguished NAFEM "Merit Award." He served as corporate member of the Rochester Methodist Hospital at the Mayo Clinic. A director of the Dairy and Food Industries Supply Assoc. for 30 years, Joe also served as President, and is the recipient of their esteemed "Bronze Plaque" award.

Honored in 1981 as Wisconsin Small Business Person of the Year, Joe served as director of the Sparta Union National Bank & Trust Co., and on the Board of Directors of the Wisconsin Assoc. of Manufacturers and Commerce. He was county chairman of a major political party, is past president of the Sparta Chamber of Commerce, and has served his home city as Mayor.

Common Sense and Plain Dealing

By Joe Larson

*Nothing astonishes men so much as
common sense and plain dealing.*
                    - Ralph Waldo Emerson

Emerson said that way back in the 19th century. Sometimes I'm surprised to discover how many things we've forgotten about — ideas that worked well for a long time but aren't used any more just because they're old. Maybe we've simply gotten tired of hearing about them.

It's true that a few simple principles that were good fifty years ago will still be good a hundred years from now, and it could be that the application of some good old-fashioned common sense to today's business world could contribute as much as a heap of management courses from the best business schools.

Common sense is most valuable when disaster strikes. A tragic fire destroyed our Sparta Brush Company plant and warehouse in 1980. At first we were in shock as we surveyed the damage, a loss of more than one million dollars.

But four months later we were back in operation with full production. It was our Sparta Brush employees' cooperation, and dedicated efforts, their common sense in the handling of this terrible situation that immediately made the difference.

Our community of Sparta, Wisconsin supported us with "an opportunity to act." Our suppliers all called with offers to assist. We took Will Shakespeare's advice: We "Screwed up our courage to the sticking place," and wasted not a moment on vain regrets.

We began in the first hour to rebuild. I believe it is not important what happens to us, it is how we respond that really counts. When Notre Dame University burned, Father Sorin, its founder, picked up a stick and was moving it in the dirt. Someone said sadly, "He is trying to salvage something."

Father Sorin replied, "Hand me a shovel! I'm laying out the new building." Tom Edison used almost the same words when his workshop burned. Common sense is beginning at once to rebuild.

I've never turned my back on good old common sense: I've been leaning on and learning from the examples of other people's common sense since I was a kid growing up in a small town in west-central Wisconsin. Back in those days, when households had iceboxes instead of electric refrigerators, there was an ice company in our town. The ice house was located at the edge of the lake, and it was the custom to hold the annual ice harvest during the Christmas holidays so the schoolboys could help. Men would be hired to cut the ice, and young lads would be paid to crawl around inside the icehouse, packing sawdust between the big ice cakes. There would usually be eight or ten young fellows carrying heavy bushel baskets of sawdust back under those low beams and tucking it in around the ice. I was one of them. It was very hard work.

After my first morning on the job I walked home across the lake and told my mother, "I just can' t do it. My back is killing me."

My mother didn't say a word. She fed me some lunch and let me lie down a few minutes. Then she took me by the ear, marched me over to the top of the hill and said, "You get back there!"

Well, I went back and to my surprise, that afternoon was a snap! I had gotten my second wind.

I had also learned a basic lesson in life. Had my mother let me give up that day, I wouldn't have known the pride or the satisfaction of success. I put a lot of stock in past experience, out of necessity and out of choice.

Applied Knowledge

I was not able to finish high school. I was a dropout before the word was even coined. My mother had been widowed back in the '30s, and in those days a widow's pension didn't go very far. Completing high school became a luxury we couldn't afford.

Thus, I was very young when I realized that nothing would come easy, and that if I wanted something I was going to have to work for it. I had to develop the self-discipline to get up in the morning and put in a full day's work. It never occurred to me to feel bad about not being able to go on in school, and attribute this to my mother's good old-fashioned common sense.

My mother used to tell me about a young neighbor whose husband wanted to do nothing but go to school. He took course after course, stopping now and then to teach somewhere for a year or two before moving on to study at yet another school. His wife worked to support him in a dozen different towns.

One day they came to call on my mother, who was then in her sixties. She was out working in her garden, and she tried unsuccessfully to get this young fellow to help her. As she told me later, "Why, he's been going to school all his life, and he doesn't even know how to hold a hoe!"

That pointed out another lesson for me. Knowledge isn't of any use if you can't apply it. A lot of people blessed with a formal education are unable to apply their knowledge once they've left the academic halls. That's a tragic waste of good, qualified people.

You can't expect to accomplish something in life by simply conjuring up a list of goals. You have to have a mind that isn't lazy and a back to match, so that when an opportunity presents itself you'll be prepared to take advantage of it.

The Paths of Opportunity

I've often been asked if my success might not be due to mere luck. I used to wonder about that: Is there some force that plucks certain people out of the ordinary course of events and directs them instead toward worthwhile acomplishments?

Certainly some people believe in fate. Not I. I believe that a person who has worked hard and accumulated all the necessary information *is ready to take advantage* of opportunity. I believe that there will be a crossing of paths — the right chance at the right time — and the fellow who had done his homework *will recognize the opportunity and act.*

These paths of opportunity meet many times in our lives. But many of us fail to recognize them when we stand right at the intersection.

Looking back on my life I can see where I took advantage of opportunities as they came along. I was in the right place at the right time, and, more important, I *acted* at the right time. I was early blessed with a sense of my life's direction. While most boys my age were dreaming of growing up to be aviators, I saw myself as a businessman. Furthermore, I was already gaining experience — I was always trying to sell something, whether it was newspapers, Watkins products, or baby chicks.

I was drawn into business because it was fun for me. I like to talk. I was a natural-born storyteller. Speech was my favorite class in high school. And when company came to visit I monopolized the conversation until my mother sent me off to bed.

Liking people and enjoying good talk made me a natural-born salesman. And every successful businessman must first be a salesman, for it is *he* who really sells the stuff: A company president must *sell the employees* on the product, and on the idea that if they produce, and produce well, everyone benefits — the customers, the company, and the workers. Everyone in the plant, right on down the line, must be sold *before* the selling job extends to the salespeople who distribute the product.

The Bright Light of Wit

Another gift of great importance to me is an appreciation of humor. I believe that the Lord gave us humor for the same reason that the automobile manufacturers in Detroit put shock absorbers under a car and foam rubber in the seat cushions.

There's great value in not being too thin-skinned or too quick to take offense. It's been said that humor is the best way for people to keep their problems from overwhelming them. Turning the bright light of wit on a problem lessens the hold it has on us and makes it seem small enough to overcome.

Doing Your Best

I also think it's helpful to be able to picture yourself in a particular role, to know what is expected of you, and most important, to recognize what you expect of yourself.

I remember the heavy financial responsibility I had when I was still a boy. My father's long illness had made it necessary to take out a mortgage on our house. By today's standards it was a small mortgage, $800 at five percent interest. But every year we had to get that $40 together to pay the interest. (I still remember walking up to the big house on the hill with that money clutched in my hand.)

The year I had earned that interest money myself by picking apples — I was thirteen or so — we learned that my sister needed an operation. Those were the days before health insurance, and her husband had no alternative but to borrow the money from us. He promised to repay us before the mortgage payment was due, but as the deadline approached I began to imagine those people coming down from the hill and taking our house away from us. But the money arrived, just on the day it was due.

That traumatic wait taught me another valuable lesson. It strengthened my natural inclination toward optimism and reminded me that there is an inner peace that comes with knowing you've done your best. It heralded my basic business philosophy:

Nobody has ever made a success out of security; there are times when one must take a chance.

Crossroads

That philosophy stood me in good stead in 1939, when I was eighteen and working for the Works Progress Administration. I was part of a crew sent out to hunt the hills for barberry bushes, the host plant for the rust that was damaging the local grain crop. I wasn't too happy doing that, but it meant income of $39 a month.

A fellow was allowed to pick up other work if he could. So in my spare time I sold baby chicks to the farmers who lived along those roads.

At the same time we had a roomer at our house, a student at the local teachers' college who was a Fuller Brush man on the side. The National Guard and the Army Reserves were activated that year, and he was one of those called up. Before he left he convinced me that I should take over his Fuller Brush territory.

I remember going down to the post office where the fellows were met by the WPA truck each morning. When I told them that I was quitting to go out selling Fuller brushes they just roared. They thought I was out of my mind to give up the security of $39 a month in order to do something that had never before made anyone a success.

But for me it was the crossroad, the time for action based on the experience I had. Their laughter made me all the more determined to dare to be different. My defiance carried me through the first two weeks, when I had to do all my selling on foot.

At that time I was averaging about $100 a week. That gave me enough confidence to march down to the car dealer and announce that I had to have a car. Since I had no money, I offered to leave my shotgun as collateral. They wouldn't accept the shotgun, but they did give me a Model A for $75. Six months later I traded it in for a '37 Ford.

My district included Minnesota and Wisconsin. I won so many sales awards in my area that my boss came to me and said, "Joe, we're going to ask you a favor. We'll give you a prize, but we're going to take you out of the contest. Everybody says that there's no use in trying because Larson wins 'em all, anyway."

Training and Timing

I think my success then came from the fact that I was developing the good business habit of always looking for a better way to do things. Accordingly, when the opportunity arose I took a two-week sales course with the Jewel Tea Company, although Fuller Brush persuaded me to return to work for them.

Shortly afterward, the country began to mobilize for war in earnest. I left sales work to help construct a nearby Army camp. Married, with a family, I was still ineligible for the draft.

And once again the formula of training plus timing presented itself. The very day the Army construction job closed, a friend employed by Jewel Tea Company mentioned that they were looking for an area salesman. I referred to the two-week training course I had completed, and I was hired on the spot. There I stayed until the Selective Service sent me my official "Greetings."

During my experiences on the road I learned some basic concepts that have helped me ever since. I learned that I had to make so many calls a day and that I had to always be on time. The women to whom I sold wanted to be able to set their clocks by me, and if I got behind not only was my schedule thrown off, but I was thought to be undependable.

I learned that if you are to sell quality you must *believe* in quality, that if you attempt to economize with cheaper service in just one little corner of your business, it's bound to show sooner or later.

My attention to dependability and quality service paid well, for when I returned home from the Air Corps, Jewel Tea Company had a job waiting for me. There then occurred another remarkable example of training and timing in my business life. A local shopkeeper suggested that I look into a line of men's footwear which promised a good future in sales. I arranged for an interview, took the necessary tests, and was told that I soon would be hearing from the company.

Two months later, on a Saturday morning, they called to say that I could start work immediately. But they were just twenty-four hours too late. The previous afternoon I had bought the Sparta Brush Company!

Dare to be Different

Everyone thought I was out of my mind to buy that rundown company. But I was encouraged by the business factors that I had come to rely upon and I was blessed with the optimism of a fellow not yet turned thirty: I could dare to be different. I knew I had the self-discipline to work hard, and I had a history of experience in the field. I saw it as the crossing of two paths — the right chance at the right time. I recognized that it was the time to seize the opportunity and to act.

I saw promise in the little dairy brush factory,

run until then by a couple of nice old folks. I was not discouraged by the fact that it had been in the path of a disastrous flood, that what bristles were left had been damaged by water, and that the machinery was pretty well shot.

My wife Esther nearly suffered a nervous breakdown at the thought of my leaving a secure job for such a gamble, but with her help we persevered. The first two or three years were a real trial. We did a lot of experimenting. We were determined to achieve and preserve quality. I was on the road from Monday through Friday, and I worked in the factory on Saturday and Sunday.

Two-Way Trust

After selling direct we began to realize that if we were to grow we would need a nationwide jobber distribution arrangement. We realized, too, that we would have to establish some basic principles, so that our customers would recognize and appreciate that we would not sell direct.

We developed a written creed called "We Believe," in which we clearly established the roles to be followed by us, the manufacturer, and by our right arm — the reputable jobber. We acknowledged our responsibility to create products of consistently high quality, and we recognized the need for the jobber to supply his customers the service and counseling necessary for excellence in our product's performance. Some of our jobbers still have that creed hanging on their walls.

We developed a two-way display of trust which enabled both factory and jobber to excel in service. We supported our jobbers with vigorous trade-paper advertising and promotion and sales aids. We listened to their suggestions.

And we saw further that if we were going to serve the best interests of the dairy industry — once more hearkening back to the lesson I had learned as a boy — we were going to have to pay our share of the rent. We were going to have to be active in the industry's associations.

We joined.

Back in 1952 we were probably one of the smallest companies in the industry to join the Dairy and Food Industries Supply Association. The cost of the initiation fee and the first year's dues were so substantial that I had to borrow on my life insurance. (Nobody ever made a success out of security!)

Membership in the D.F.I.S.A. gave us the privilege of exhibiting in the big exposition. And I realized at those first large conventions that I wasn't going to learn anything by standing on the sidelines. I had to get acquainted with people.

I profited a great deal in those early years by listening to the older, successful people in the dairy industry. I went out of my way to ask them questions, and if I didn't get the right answers I concluded that I hadn't asked the right questions. It was an educational experience not available in books or in the classroom. I took all the information I could get back home with me, where I tried to adapt it to my own business.

It surprised me to discover that some members did not become involved. They were content to sit on the sidelines, asking why this or that had not happened, never realizing that it was because they had not volunteered to help.

In those early days I complained whenever I objected to something. That would result in my being appointed to a committee, where it was felt that I would be quiet! But with my love of conversation, I wound up as chairman, and was then elected a director. I went on to become president of the association.

I was in awe the first time I sat at a board of directors' meeting. The average company represented on the board of the D.F.I.S.A. employed 400 or 500 people. Our little company had only 10 employees then. Most of the board members were products of prestigious eastern schools; many were presidents of dairy equipment companies that employed upwards of 2,000 people.

At that moment I got my second breath, the way I had that winter when my mother sent me back to the icehouse. It was then that I knew for certain that I could come from a background of limited education, take a small company with a good product and a good reputation, and with the right kind of thinking and energetic exposure, accomplish the American dream.

Daring to be different has become a kind of slogan for me and for our company We are indeed serious about making the best. Shortly before the fire my son Jack and I visualized a machine that would greatly improve the quality and the production of a particular type of brush. We traveled to Germany to meet with the designers and were told that no such machine existed. We replied that we were convinced such a machine was possible, and that the only reason one had not been built before was that no one had had the conviction to order an unproven $100,000 machine.

That machine took a year-and-a-half to construct. It is now successfully in use and performing beyond our expectations, and we have the satisfaction of knowing that it will take time for any competitor to catch up with us. (Nobody has ever made a success out of security!)

I am reminded of a poem written by a friend and neighbor of mine from Scottsdale, Arizona. She, too, was never satisfied with mediocrity. Neither age nor failing health dimmed her spirit or lessened her appreciation of life. She wrote this poem about the subject of achievement:

> *Ten men reach a canyon;*
> *Nine will hesitate;*
> *But one will build a simple bridge*
> *To bear his body's weight.*
>
> *The land ahead is shadowy,*
> *Obscure, as in a dream.*
> *Nine men see the darkness:*
> *One man sees a gleam.*

He summons up his courage,
    He subjugates his fear,
As, by himself, he mounts the bridge
    To face a new frontier.

And so he crosses over
    To alien lands unknown.
Uncertainties assail him as he
    Stands there all alone.

His body says, "Stop dreaming!
    Go back from whence you came!"
His spirit says, "Don't listen,"
    And sets the bridge aflame.

                  - Eleanor Neissl

RICHARD D. MC CALL, Ph.D.
1019 University Tower Building
Little Rock, AR 72204

Richard D. McCall, Ph.D.

Richard D. McCall, Ph.D., the developer of Warrior Concepts Unlimited business excellence programs, is founder and director of the Human Performance Institute, one of the nation's leading performance enhancement consulting firms. As a behavorial management consultant and clinical hypnotherapist, he has developed numerous highly acclaimed performance enhancement systems for business, health, and sports applications!

Dr. McCall is a clinical member of the International Stress/Tension Control Society, the American Guild of Hypnotherapists and the Association to Advance Ethical Hypnosis. He is a professional member of the American Society for Training and Development and the National Speakers Association. A master martial arts instructor, holding a 5th degree black belt in Japanese Karate and Bushido, Dr. McCall has studied Asian philosophy, human behavior and communication sciences with leading universities throughout the country, earning his degree in Applied Psychology.

A much sought-after speaker and seminar trainer, Dr. McCall and his uniquely different personal excellence concepts have been featured in numerous publications and talk shows and was listed in the l983-84 "Who's Who In Professional Sports" and the l985-86 "Who's Who In American Martial Arts." Originally raised in the Japanese culture, he now makes his home in Little Rock, Arkansas, where he writes, teaches martial arts and maintains his private behavioral management practice.

Warrior Concepts Unlimited
The Education of a Business Samurai

By Richard D. McCall, Ph.D.

*"The FUTURE of business excellence is
emerging from 700 years in the PAST!"*

As I sat on the large, flat boulder that summer morning as a youth, there was a cool wetness to the air as it touched my face, as is common in the mountain regions of Japan. The sun was just beginning to make its slow ascent above the horizon, and the streamers of golden light pierced beautifully through the remaining foggy mist of night. It was a peaceful and inspiring scene, yet, even more inspiring was the way the radiant light illuminated the calm, restful face of the swordmaster who knelt before me. There was a sudden sense of timelessness... as if I had been thrust back 700 years into Japan's warrior-rich past!

Looking at my *sensei*, from my vantage point on the rock, I could barely detect the smooth, yet deliberate pattern of his breathing as he sat on his knees in the traditional *seiza* position of the samurai warrior. Poised in his left hand was the 300 year old *katana*, or samurai sword, razor sharp and still nestled in its long polished scabbard. His back was straight, his head erect and there was a quiet intensity and clearness in his eyes. He stared straight ahead at a small overhang of leaves directly in front of him, without the slightest hint of distraction.

Only then did I begin to realize what my mentor had been so intensely concentrating upon since the beginning of daybreak. As the sun rose and shone through the foliage, it produced a silvery halo around each leaf, where the dew and fog had begun to settle and condense, and it was apparent that *sensei* had become focused upon one leaf in particular. A delicate orb of moisture had been slowly forming and preparing to fall from the tip of the leaf. As the droplet grew larger, there was also a feeling of impending action, *as if lightning were about to strike!*

And then it happened! The dewdrop began to fall, and the previously quiet and serene *bugeisha sensei* became a blur of movement and energy! As he launched forward onto his right leg, there was a sound of sucking air as the blade sped, at what seemed like the speed of light, towards its falling target! As if it were its destiny, the glistening tip of the *katana* sliced dramatically through the drop of water, instantly converting it back into the mist from which it had come!

As the blade completed its cutting arc, the master effortlessly twirled the sword between his fingers, reversing its direction of travel, and then returned it to the *saya,* or scabbard, as swiftly as it had been drawn. Within an instant, *sensei* was back in the kneeling *seiza* again, breathing smoothly and deliberately, as if nothing had transpired!

It was then that I felt an overwhelming rush of awe, respect and admiration flood throughout my entire being! With it was an intense feeling of desire to totally dedicate my time and energies to understanding, and if possible, mastering, the tradition-rich discipline and way of life of the legendary samurai warrior. It is a feeling that has never left me since that moment, twenty some-odd years ago... a feeling that has shaped my life, my character and my personal sense of honor and self-identity. It is a feeling that has given me an element of "control" over my fate and destiny, and enabled me to discard the notion of "luck" in successful living! And it is a feeling I strive to share with everyone I meet, whether it be in my personal life or in my professional work as a behavioral management consultant and martial arts instructor.

Warfare and Daily Living

During the many years I have studied Japanese philosophy and martial arts, I have had the privilege of studying under several outstanding master instructors, all of whom were direct descendants of the original samurai. These men were not fanatics or eccentric. They were solid, sincere and *successful* business professionals who truly understood the nature of conflict in the real world we live in. They could see the immediate and direct applicability of the strategies and psychology of the warrior knights of historical Japan to everyday situations and needs. They recognized the universal thread of "warfare" that runs through every human endeavor and negotiation, whether it be personal or professional.

Think about it for a moment. When was the last time *you* were in a fight? If your imagination and memory carried you back to a time in the fifth grade when the playground bully bloodied your nose, then you're probably mistaken! In fact it probably wasn't even as long ago as last week! It was probably this morning, or maybe a few minutes ago! Sounds strange doesn't it? Then perhaps it would help if we looked at the situation from a *different point of view!*

"When you see ORDINARY situations with EXTRAORDINARY insight, it is like finding a JEWEL in the rubbish!"   - Samurai Slogan

We are brought up to believe that fighting is

the *exception* in life, a once in a while thing, when all along it has been *the rule!* Like it or not, life **IS** a martial art! But where, you ask, are the punches, grabs, kicks and weapons we so commonly associate with *actual* combat? Well, let's see.

As our society has evolved and matured, so have our methods of acquiring dominance and gain. It is no longer acceptable to carry *physical* weapons or to maintain menacing stances. Instead, we now manifest and exert our strength and will upon each other through words, looks, facts, figures and complex negotiations. To some, this may not resemble warfare, but it is *warfare*, none the less!

This is most evident in the tremendous toll this *non-warfare* takes on our emotional and physical lives! We have become a stress-plagued society in which people turn to drugs, alcohol and other destructive forms of "recreation" to help mend their "wounds" and burnt-out emotions. Yes, life and business is *warfare*, and we are all warriors by *necessity!* The legendary warriors of Japan and each generation of successors since, have understood that we have all been thrust into this arena with little choice and with even *less* information regarding how to deal with it! Therefore, it was their belief, as it is mine, that to come out successfully happy, it would be to everyone's advantage to explore the realm of *Bushido - the WAY of the samurai warrior!*

The Warrior Knights of Japan

Few countries have had a warrior tradition as long and exciting as that of Japan. It is a tradition manifested particularly in the image of the romantic, loyal and self-sacrificing knight of ancient Japan, the samurai! He was the valiant lone swordsman whose skills, spirit and dedication were awed and respected across the land. The ultimate individual warrior, he was also the esthete, the poet, the philosopher seeing and appreciating the beauty of the cherry blossom and possessing the insight to compare its short stay on earth to his own short but meaningful life.

It was the samurai's destiny to be the commander of soldiers on the battlefield by day, the stealthy messenger of justice by night, the keeper of peace and the aristocratic administrator. Then, paradoxically, he was also the teacher of social culture, etiquette, literature, art and spirituality to the children. In short, the samurai warrior represented the epitome of what humankind is capable of achieving when we are willing to do so!

The Education of a Business Samurai

Even without an in-depth dissertation of the skills and accomplishments of the warrior knights of Japan, it is safe to say that the world has rarely seen anything to match the elite mentality demonstrated in the samurai tradition. And let's take our imagination a step further and pretend that we could transport, forward in time, one of these professional warriors to this day and age. Then we would send him through an MBA program at Harvard, after which we would set him up in business in a "Fortune 500" company. How do you suppose he would do?

Whether he worked in sales, management, human resources development or any other area of the corporate structure, you can imagine the tremendous impact his unique mentality and warrior strategies would have upon his associates, his company and his career! His performance appraisal would probably read: "He is absolutely fearless; a real team leader; a super self-motivator and an example to his associates; honest and honorable beyond description; appears to be willing to *die* for what he believes in, which makes him a powerful negotiator; outstanding attendance with no sick days; currently breaking all previous production records."

Wouldn't *you* like to be like that modern "business samurai"? Well, you *can* be, and you don't need a time machine to accomplish this feat, either!

Oriental wisdom is timeless, and knows no social, cultural or economic boundaries. By simply looking closely at the fundamentals of the philosophy, psychology and concepts of the samurai, and doing so with an *open mind,* you will discover, as I have, that they are applicable to *any situation,* and with the spirit and energy they instill in you, your possibilities for success in life become *unlimited!*

Warrior Concepts Unlimited

The main feature of samurai training that made it special and unique, was that it treated the warrior holistically — as a whole person, mind, body and spirit. It recognized that when one goes into battle, their skill with the sword or any other tool or resource is inseparable from what he or she is experiencing subjectively, inside their mind and body! If there is fear, worry or self-doubt, the fighter's performance will be directly and inevitably affected. And if the warrior is *terrified,* he or she may never even set foot on the battlefield, but might well run away — as do many individuals today, who let opportunity slip by because they are too scared to try!

Our attitudes — towards the battle, ourselves and our chances of coming out victorious — *directly* and *powerfully* affect our outward performance. From this sensible observation came my emphasis of training modern business warriors on two levels of development — the *outer* and the *inner* levels!

"To subdue the enemy that comes leaping at you, your body, spirit and weapon MUST be perfectly POISED!" - Samurai Maxim

Outer development concerns perfecting the warrior's technical skills with the body, weapons, tools or other *external* resources available to him or her. The salesperson, whose adeptness can be *visibly* seen in skillful probing, handling of resistance and then closing the sale, have their outer skills down pat. Formal business education — the kind received at universities, schools and seminaries — is what the samurai would call *outer training* in technique.

Inner development, on the other hand, is of an entirely different nature. If you were asked to choose between possessing great technical business ability *or* an unconquerable spirit, which would *you* choose? Neither the samurai nor the Japanese businessman of today would have any problem deciding. Without hesitation they would choose *spirit,* the *inner* strength, also called the *Zen* of warriorship.

This unfortunately, is the greatly neglected side of modern business education. Business *is* warfare, yet our society, with its western, somewhat superficial perspective of productivity and achievement, all but ignores this critically important area of *inner development!*

"Success will ALWAYS by yours when your heart and mind are without DISTURBANCE!"
-Miyamoto Musashi (1584-1645)

In modern Japan, even today, the inner, subjective side of the person is considered of far more importance to performance than technical skill. Whatever the field — business, politics, sports or the arts — the inner dimensions of personality, such as courage, commitment and honor— in short, the person's *spirit,* is considered primary! Person *first,* technique *second!*

"*Your sword and spirit must be united!*" "*Behind every strong technique must be an even stronger spirit!*" "*He who understands true warriorship can subdue ten opponents with his spirit alone!*" — these are just a few of the countless references to be found in samurai writing as to the immense importance, in battle, of what you are as a person... your *inner* self.

So *can* a person be trained to overcome fear and hesitancy? *Is* courage learnable? *Can* someone acquire self-confidence and boldness in action, even late in life? Is it *possible* for someone to pick up the ability to leap forward against even the most formidable of foes? The answer to such questions is undeniably found within the realm of samurai warrior concepts... and the answer is always *YES!*

The Four Components of Modern Warriorship

As I have mentioned before, there is a distinct "common thread" that runs through all forms of warfare and conflict. My many years of study in the Japanese martial arts is what led me, originally, into the field of human behavioral management. As a professional consultant and as a martial arts instructor, I have been blessed with the opportunity to meet and work with over ten thousand people from all walks of life. I feel confident in saying that I have seen, or been consulted on, every form of conflict and warfare imaginable.

Although my clinical education and experience have certainly been helpful in resolving many cases, more often than not, it was the wisdom, philosophy and insight passed along to me by my Japanese *sensei* (teachers) that has aided me the most in assisting my clients and students in developing lasting solutions for their problems.

In light of these observations, in my seminars and in "business warrior" retreats I have conducted, I have subdivided modern warriorship training into four components: (1) *Success Motivation,* (2) *Mental Excellence,* (3) *Communication, and* (4) *Physical Wellness.*

While each of these components is equally important in the total scheme of understanding true business warriorship, I have arranged them in logical order, the first two of which are for *inner development* and the second two for *outer development.*

1. Success Motivation: "The Bushido Spirit"

My master once told me the story of a wise old samurai and one of his students who went for a walk through the countryside. The student pointed to a fox chasing a rabbit and said, "Oh, the poor rabbit!" The old master then said, "The rabbit will elude the fox." The student seemed surprised and responded, "But master, you see, the fox is faster!" "The rabbit will get away," calmly repeated the master. "What makes you so sure?" asked the student. The master confidently replied, "Because the fox is simply running for his dinner, but the rabbit... he is running for *HIS LIFE!*"

"It is the reality of DEATH that gives LIFE its richest meaning!"   -Samurai Maxim

Many a great philosopher has asked the question, "What would you have done *differently* today, if you knew beyond a doubt that you were going to die tomorrow?" A morbid question, some might think, but a *valuable* one,
if you would take a moment to consider it seriously.

Perhaps you would have been extra attentive to your family. Maybe you would have called an old friend you haven't talked to in many years. It is likely that God would have seemed a little more real and personal to you. Perhaps you would have reflected, with a sense of regret, upon the things you never quite got around to doing or accomplishing. You might have even gone out there and tried to get the last "big sale" you were previously intimidated about attempting, and *got it!* Why? Because you approached the situation with a powerfully unique "it's now or never" attitude!
The examples given above reflect the true essence of *bushido,* and some of the exciting life changes

that are experienced by those who adopt it into their scheme of living!

Zen - a Fresh Look Through an Old Window

The samurai warrior lived with a vivid awareness of death and his mortality, and it gave his daily life a fresh new meaning. Philosophically, he accepted death as a natural and inevitable part of living, but it served him as a constant reminder of his true priorities and goals. In the western world we tend to hide from the reality of death, to assume the attitude that it is just something that happens to the other guy, and for that reason, we *lose out.*

The essence of *Zen* and *bushido* is to look at life from a different angle every chance we get, to fully experience each situation and take each opportunity as if there were *no tomorrow!* In this way you begin to live life for the sake of the moment, rather than just blankly staring at the "big picture." The need for constant excitation, incentive bonuses and other external forms of motivation to make you want to get out there and "get it," diminishes dramatically. Each day you find yourself awakening to an exciting new adventure, instead of just "another day" at the office or in the field.

The spirit of *bushido* tends to also awaken your senses and your awareness of the world around you, like the blind man who has just regained his sight! Life can become seriously monotonous if we let it, and most people do let it! There is an old *Zen* adage that says, "Wherever you are, *be there!*" This, too is the essence of *bushido.*

The spirit of *bushido* and *Zen* are referred to as many things — a philosophy, a psychology of action, grounded on decisiveness, spontaneity, strength of will, adaptability, courage and bravery! It was this psychological aspect which appealed most to the samurai. It served to give him the kind of power and strength he needed to *win,* just as it can today for you and me, their modern-day counterparts.

To rush forward and confidently face the enemy, even if death might await him, he needed what the *bushido spirit* taught — to live from the gut level, to act without holding back, without reservation and with *total commitment!* It gave him, as it can us, a fresh look through an old window!

2. Mental Excellence: "Inner-Warrior Cybernetics"

Since the mid 1970's, a new field of study has emerged upon the business and behavioral psychology scene — that of peak-performance training. Human resources development is probably one of the most important advances made in the past decade, in understanding how to get the *most* from our potential!

We are told by behavioral scientists that the

human mind is like a super-computer, that it is programmable and, more importantly, that it is *re-programmable*. Superlearning systems, autogenics classes, self-hypnosis programs and other "mental cybernetics" concepts, are now being used by people from all walks of life, in an attempt to get more from their minds and inner potential. But is this actually a *new* idea? Not really, as you will see!

The eastern world has always tended to be inner-training oriented, as was the samurai, in particular. Quiet periods of meditation and prayer were an automatic part of their daily ritual. For the warrior who constantly faced the reality of death, it has an absolutely *vital* role in maintaining a sense of harmony and peace within themselves — harmony in mind, body and spirit!

Modern science tells us that our subconscious minds rule and regulate all of our actions, emotions and fears. For this reason it is imperative for *all* warriors, whether they be historical or contemporary, to develop the ability and *habit* of "communicating" our philosophies, beliefs and goals to the inner consciousness.

Warrior Meditation Has Three Purposes

Any good program or book on relaxation or autogenic training can help you to get the mind more receptive for effective warrior meditation. The technique used is simply a matter of preference. What *is important*, however, is the purpose and application of the meditation!   The three main objectives should be to: *(l) rest and prepare the body, (2) focus the mind on the bushido spirit, and (3) renew and enhance your spiritual strength.*

In the opening section of this writing, I relived with you a very special moment I shared with my *sensei* one summer morning, a long time ago. It took me many years to fully appreciate what I had witnessed that day, but I have since come to realize that he had vividly and dramatically demonstrated the three elements of meditation, in their purest form.

"Rest and Prepare the BODY!"

My master had been kneeling in a position known as *seiza*, a position very common in the Japanese culture. His back was straight, head erect and there was a *quiet intensity* in his eyes. His breathing was smooth and deliberate.

Quieting the body always leads to quieting of the mind, and it isn't necessary to lie down to do it. *Sensei* had learned through practice, as did his samurai ancestors, that one can accomplish "rest" in *any* setting or situation. An invaluable skill such as this afforded him, as it does you and I, the opportunity to instantly focus the mind and spirit whenever and wherever the need arises.

Focus the MIND on the Bushido Spirit!"

The *bushido spirit* teaches us to be in harmony with who and all that is around us. As he knelt and focused his mind on his objective, *sensei* developed a sense of "oneness" with the ancient sword, which was poised in readiness in his hand, with the air and sunshine which touched his face, with the leaf, upon which the drop of dew was slowly forming... and finally and importantly, with the *dewdrop itself!*

He was imagining, *in advance,* the path of the blade as it would pass through the center of the drop as it fell. Everything else on earth was completely unimportant, as he prepared for that impending moment when the drop would finally descend... totally ready to act swiftly and effectively when that moment arrived, which it soon *did.* He was communicating his sense of *bushido spirit* to his inner consciousness and was creating a joint destiny for himself, the blade, and the droplet of water.

We, as modern business samurai, can also create such a destiny between ourselves, our prospective clients and *success,* through the amazing power of *our* subconscious *inner-warrior!*

"Renew and Enhance Your SPIRITUAL Strength"

The Japanese word for spiritual strength is *Ki.* It is the energy from which all things come, the energy that binds all things and events together and gives them substance. Many have called it the "life-force." To the warrior, it has a *real* and *tangible* substance. As in the movie "Star Wars" (which, incidentally, depicts a futuristic version of the samurai warrior and the spirit of *bushido*), it is the "force" that flows through each of us, our eternal connection to the creator. The more aware of this energy we are or become, the *more* it will work with us and for us.

As he prepared to act, my master was getting "in-tune" with his *Ki*, which in turn would provide him with near super-human strength and courage to accomplish almost *anything!* Historically, the tremendous power and feats of skill of the legendary samurai warrior cannot be denied. You and I, as modern business samurai, can learn from their ancient, time-tested concepts in mental excellence, and more fully tap and develop our *inner-warrior* potential!

3. Communication: "Verbal Self-Defense"

The previous two "warrior concepts" have dealt with the all-important area of *inner development*. In the real world of business and daily living, however, *outer development,* the perfection of the technical skills of our trade, are also essential. The most powerful and frequently used "weapon" of the modern day business samurai is that of the *spoken word.* Communication skills in modern business warriorship are equally as important as swordsmanship was to the historical samurai. Even the great "sword-saint" of ancient Japan, Miyamoto Musashi once said, *"The tongue can be sharper and more piercing than the finest sword!"* And how right he was!

There are three facets inherent to all interpersonal communication: (1) the *visual* facet, which is body language, mannerisms and expressions; (2) the *vocal* facet, or the tone of voice, inflection and rhythm and use; and (3) the *verbal* facet, consisting of the actual words and phrases you say. Since communication is actually such a *physical* discipline, it can be easily paralleled with physical martial art training, which I have broken down into five categories of proficiency. Although it would take more space than we have here to cover all of the aspects of each of these areas of training, I would nonetheless like to give you an interesting *overview*, from the samurai's point of view:

Category #1: A proper peacekeeping attitude

Samurai maxim: *"To fight and conquer in 100 battles is NOT the highest skill... to subdue the enemy WITHOUT A FIGHT, that is the HIGHEST skill!* The idea here is obvious. The objective in any confrontation is to resolve the issue as efficiently as possible, and this means *de-escalating* the situation. We must seek to eliminate our ego and flinch reactions in dealings with people, and instead, rely upon our personal sense of confidence and self-esteem. We should train ourselves, in *any* type of confrontation, to *respond* rather than *react!*

Category #2: Proper breath control

Samurai maxim: *"If you know the art of breathing, you will possess the strength, wisdom and courage of TEN TIGERS!"* It is interesting to note, that in most verbal confrontations, the average person will either pant or hold their breath. For proper self-control, *neither* of these is appropriate. The first thing I teach a new student of martial arts is that they *must breath* as they act. Breathing properly while you engage your opponent enables you to maintain a sense of composure in your expressions and body language, and to ultimately take control of the situation effectively and power-fully!

Category #3: Strong stances

Samurai maxim: *"To subdue the opponent that comes leaping at you, your spirit, MIND and BODY must be perfectly POISED!"* In warfare there are two kinds of stances — *physical* and *attitudinal*. In communication it is important to build a strong foundation of power at both levels, since both will contribute dramatically to your personal courage, power and effectiveness! Becoming aware of your personal stability and body language during tense or threatening communication will help you to become a more *rooted* and *unshakeable* business warrior!

Category #4: Aikijutsu

Samurai maxim: *"When attacked straight and*

hard, respond SOFT and CIRCULAR; when attacked soft and circular, penetrate STRAIGHT and HARD1" Aikijutsu is a Japanese word meaning "to find harmony within conflict." In any martial art, including verbal self-defense, it is the most advanced and effective concept you can learn. It is a principle of using the aggressor's *own* strength, anger and energy against them to *re-direct* the attack in a harmless direction, with *minimal violence!* All skillful communicators and diplomats know of the principle of *aikijutsu,* although they may have never heard the term. It is a warrior skill based upon timing rhythm, emotional self-control and level-headed thinking in the heat of battle. It is a concept that anyone can learn and master, requiring only practice and a willingness to learn. The cuts and slashes of business warfare are administered by the spoken word, and it should be a high priority of every modern samurai to learn how to deflect and harmlessly parry the verbal advances of the opposition!

Category #5: Maintenance of focus

Samurai maxim: *"The warrior must be always SINGLE-MINDED, with one objective in mind — to subdue the enemy and defend the CAUSE, looking neither backwards nor sideways!"* The objective of this category is to maintain a sense of direction and purpose when under attack. It is imperative that the business samurai remain "focused" upon the objective of the communication, and not become confused or sidetracked by the attitude, actions or comments of the opponentss. In this way we remain firmly in control throughout the conflict, and able to produce the desired outcome from the encounter!

Regardless of the type of industry we work in, the five categories of martial art/communication proficiency I've briefly touched on above can be applied by *you!* "Warrior Concepts in Communication" provide the business warrior of today with the kind of confidence and adeptness in "battle" that was instrumental in making the ancient samurai legends in their own time! Now, let's take a look at the fourth component of warriorship and how it applies to the business samurai of *today!*

4. Physical Wellness: "Executive Self-Protection"

Caring for and protecting the body from harm was always one of the most important priorities of the legendary warrior knights of Japan. The body was considered a sacred temple which housed the"spirit," and was, of course, indispensable. It is just as important for the modern business samurai to care for his or her physical health and well-being. Remember, warriorship is a wholistic concept — spirit, mind *and* body! There is an old and very true slogan that goes, "You can only do as good as you *feel!*" For maximum success, modern warriorship should be a total commitment to excellence!

Accidents not withstanding, harm can only come to the body from one of two sources — either *sickness* or *attack.* For this reason, in my modern warriorship seminars and retreats, I have made it a point to include useful, practical information on fitness and nutrition in the program curriculum. With the abundance of literature and other resources available to us today on the subjects of health and fitness, the modern warrior can easily find the approach to healthy living that best suits them!

Regarding physical self-defense for the business samurai of today, it is known that the historical samurai often instructed members of the merchant class of Japan in how to use many of their "empty-hand" techniques in defense against the many roadside robbers and bandits of that time. These easy-to-learn methods of self-protection were fast, efficient and highly effective in dissuading a would-be mugger.

These techniques have been passed on through the generations and are another important part of the fascinating samurai legacy and warrior concepts, being passed on to the modern business world today, by disciples of the "Way," such as myself! The ability to defend one's self from harm, as well as those whose safety and well-being have been entrusted to us, plays an important role in developing the sense of total warriorship in the executive business professional.

The motto, *"Be prepared!"* was more than a boy scout slogan to the professional warrior! It meant to be *totally* ready — mind, body and spirit — for *any* event or circumstance that might arise in the course of daily living! This warrior concept in *physical wellness,* along with the other concepts in *success motivation, mental excellence* and *communication,* ensure the business samurai of today of a strong, unconquerable spirit and attitude... of the skill to "make peace and get results" in the war of words we engage in daily... and of the safety and good health we want and need to see our way to the *unlimited* success that will be ours, through modern business warriorship!

The "End" and the "Beginning"

In reading this overview of*Warrior Concepts Unlimited,* you have helped me to fulfill a very deep and important commitment I made to myself many years ago: To bring to the modern business world an awareness of the unlimited satisfaction, happiness and hope that the warrior concepts of the legendary samurai can bring to your career and to your life! We live in a world of conflict and warfare, but fortunately the timeless wisdom and oriental insight of these warrior knights of old can bring us out victorious, and with a resounding sense of honor and peace!

Yes the *end* draws near... but it is my hope that it is the *beginning* of a new awakening and a new adventure for you... and that you will truly discover, as I have...*that the FUTURE of business excellence IS emerging from 700 years in the PAST!*

DORIS LEE MC COY, Ph.D.
McCoy Productions
5758 Beaumont Avenue
La Jolla, CA 92037
(619)459-4971

Doris Lee McCoy, Ph.D.

Doris Lee McCoy, Ph.D., was born in Pittsburgh, earned a B.A. from Muskingum College, a Danforth Graduate Scholarship, an M.A. from Stanford University and a Ph.D. from Claremont Graduate School. She has had a private Counseling Practice, is a university professor, a speaker to business and professional groups, a television moderator/producer, author and interviewer. She moderates/produces dynamic television specials and series.

Shooting on location in Africa or interviewing top American executives, her energetic "to the heart" and crisp flair comes through. American Airlines featured her interviews for the Nightingale/Conant Corporation with Malcolm Forbes, Mary Cunningham, Philip Caldwell (former CEO of Ford Motor Co.), and Norman Cousins. Her many years in television, teaching and speaking throughout the United States, Asia, Africa and Australia qualify her as a communications specialist. High energy, professionalism and personal warmth characterize her on - and off - the screen.

She is listed in World's Who's Who of Women, *was named "Woman of the Year" by The Charter l00 and "Woman of Achievement" by the National League of American Pen Women. Dr. McCoy is a long distance swimmer, skier and mountain climber. She resides in La Jolla, California.*

The 12 Steps of Success

By Doris Lee McCoy, Ph.D.

" Happiness is something you deliver to yourself, and the way you do it is exercising your vital abilities reaching for the brass ring, not necessarily achieving it, but enjoying the level at which you do achieve. That's terribly important... to deliver... a state of happiness to oneself. A man doesn't bring that to a woman; that is something we each do for ourselves. - Norman Lear

Successful men and women. How have they done it? I have traveled throughout the United States asking over 1,000 people who are considered "successful" to answer this question. I chatted with such illuminating personalities as Helen

Hayes, Ronald Reagan, Malcolm Forbes, and Mary Kay Ash, and recorded the interviews to give others an opportunity to look into the lives of some of America's most successful people. I did not simply want to talk with these men and women as I had when some of them had appeared on my television interviews; rather, I intended to seek out some consistencies— success patterns from which I and others could benefit.

Were there complicated hurdles they had to surmount? Did some of them undergo difficult childhoods and gain from these experiences in later life? Are successful people necessarily born in a certain kind of family? Do they have a high energy level? (Sandra Day O'Connor, U.S. Supreme Court Justice, says, with a smile, "No, I don't put my feet up on the couch and eat chocolates.) Were there qualities parents could encourage in their children? Were there specific points that could help all of us to be more successful?

The answer is a resounding <u>yes</u>, there are traits consistently found in the lives of successful people. This "yes" may offer some reassurance in this day of the "crazies," with so many life styles, philosophies, new ways of doing things, even so many self-help books, that have us wondering if former beliefs are obsolete!

From my interviews with Ronald Reagan, Supreme Court Justice Sandra O'Connor, diplomat Norman Cousins, television writer/producer Norman Lear, Mary Kay Ash and many others, I have found <u>12 Steps to Success</u> or choices that these people have made to attain the goals they desired. Each successful person has their own style, and ways of making these steps their own. My hope is that you will enjoy these examples and then take the significant steps that will lead to your own success.

The definition I used to identify "SUCCESS" was broader than the popular notion of mere financial abundance and social prestige. After talking with many people who were labeled as accomplished, I concluded that real success is a high degree of fulfillment in five areas: THE MENTAL, SPIRITUAL, SOCIAL, PHYSICAL AND EMOTIONAL ASPECTS OF LIFE. I used this criteria to identify candidates for the research. I conducted interviews over a fourteen year period. The results of my research are:

THE 12 STEPS TO SUCCESS

1. Many of them choose to make the best of difficult situations and in doing so, discover more of their potential.
2. They have high self-esteem.
3. They are persistent.
4. They have a strong and active faith in God or some higher power.
5. They are decisive and self-disciplined; they know what they want.
6. They enjoy their jobs.
7. They have a sense of purpose.

8. They are in good physical health, exercise regularly and discipline themselves in their eating habits.
9. They take time away from work to relax and renew themselves.
10. Many were leaders since childhood.
11. They are androgynous
12. They take risks.

Throughout my interviews, I discovered the most often mentioned trait was:

Step#1 *"Many of them choose to make the best of difficult situations and In doing so discover more of their potential."*

Many eminent personalities overcame a negative experience or difficult situation in a positive manner, often resulting in their catapulting to greater heights. The event was powerful enough to command their attention, forcing them to consciously take charge of their lives. They were not caught up in a feeling of helplessness, but played an active role in overcoming a handicap or other personal tragedy.

It is significant to note that their characters were already sufficiently developed at the time of the crisis so that they gained strength to surmount defeat. This result might not have occurred if their ego was weak at the time of crisis. The experience also gave them an opportunity to etch their personal statement on life with deep feeling and belief.

Television writer/producer Norman Lear revealed that as he grew up, observing the marriage of his parents, he "looked at two people who lived at the top of their lungs, on the ragged ends of their nerves." In self-defense, he had to find the humor in his turbulent family situation.

As a child, Editor and UCLA Medical School professor Norman Cousins, learned the art of negotiation after an all-night experience in freezing weather: *"In my ninth year, I was pretty sickly and was sent away to a public sanitarium in New Jersey. It seems to me incredible that I was there for the short time that I was. It was only six or seven months. It would be the equivalent of a ten-year span in respect to other things. I did an awful lot of growing up in that sanitarium. Kids can be pretty rough. The second or third night I was there, in the middle of a very cold winter, [the sanitarium gang]... lifted [me] out of my bed without a blanket and dumped [me] far out in the woods and warned me not to follow them back. Kids can be cruel. Then I learned how to tame the beast. The new kids who were coming in were being beaten and tossed out too, and I just figured out a way of dealing with [the members of the gang] that gave them satisfaction in being decent. They were all very lonely and insecure... I learned a great deal about gang warfare and the ease with which kids can slide into violence and how they can win each other's esteem in terms of the cruelty they can vent."*

Never again would he fear death. What could have remained a terrifying experience fortified him with the stamina to become one of the top U.S. negotiators in major world disputes.

Florence Chadwick, record-breaking Channel swimmer, finished last in her first swimming meet. This disappointment merely propelled her to practice and try harder after that painful experience.

Many of the successful, then, accepted crises as a part of life. In some cases traumatic experience actually served as an opportunity for them to see more options than before.

Step#2. They have high self-esteem.

Norman Lear talks of building self esteem by saying: *"You like yourself. You consciously say to yourself, 'Good fellow, you said you were going to get up at eight and you did.' Feel good about the contact with the newspaper boy. You made him laugh. He made you laugh. You caught a moment with a human being. You say to yourself, 'That's terrific, good for you,' and you collect those minutes all of the time."*

I asked Lear to comment on the relationship between high self esteem and success. He replied: *"Success is how we collect our minutes. Human beings somehow, biologically or anthropologically, are constructed so that we know how to dislike ourselves when we fail ourselves. If we set the alarm clock for eight o'clock, say we're going to get up and go someplace by nine o'clock and we goof and don't leave the house, we know how to let that spoil the rest of the day. We human beings are so good at hating ourselves for goofing up little things like that... otherwise there's no way of explaining why you read constantly about a man or a woman who seems to have everything that the world deems a success — the home, the family, wealth, respectability in the community, etc. and he jumps out of a window somewhere.*

Happiness is something you deliver to your-self, and the way you do it is exercising your vital abilities reaching for the brass ring, not necessarily achieving it, but enjoying the level at which you do achieve. That's so terribly important....to deliver... a state of happiness to oneself. A man doesn't bring that to a woman; that is something we each do for ourselves"

"You turkey!" How many times have we heard a tennis player say that on missing a shot? The author of <u>Inner Tennis</u> well understood the principle of self-acceptance and attempted to teach it to tennis enthusiasts. He advised, instead of yelling "you Idiot!" at yourself when you miss a shot, to realize you are only human and instead praise yourself when you hit the ball correctly. You physically retrace the path of the racquet to "groove" the correct pattern in your memory. In the words of Norman Lear, you tell yourself, "good fellow!" And it is well established that athletes play significantly better when they imagine themselves performing correctly before competing.

One must confront one's real self before finding a healthy position from which to relate to others.

We need to honor the "unacceptable" parts we hide, as well as the pleasant, appealing parts we are quick to acknowledge. If we feel "needy" and dissatisfied, we will view other people as objects to fill our void. Using others in such a way will prevent our experiencing caring and loving relationships with them.

Step #3 They are persistent.

As Ray Kroc says: "You have to bang on doors and bang on doors and never stop!" One well-known author submitted an article for which he had a great deal of faith seventy-seven times to different publishers. It was accepted on the seventy-eighth try! His motto, attributed to Calvin Coolidge, exemplifies the course he followed throughout his life: "*Press on. Nothing in the world can take the place of persistence. Talent will not; nothing is more common than unsuccessful men with talent. Genius will not; unrewarded genius is almost a proverb. Education alone will not; the world is full of educated derelicts. Persistence and determination alone are omnipotent.*"

Persistence enables you to return to a problem over and over again, seeing it in a new light, looking for new options. The successful learn how to tap into creative new ideas by looking at familiar ones in a new way.

Letting the idea go while still being aware of the problem can be quite effective. The solution suddenly becomes clear, often after sleep, when a dream has offered a suggestion, or simply after the subconscious has had an opportunity to work on it.

Another point made by the successful was that "no" does not necessarily mean "no." Sometimes a person is just testing the waters to see what you will do next. From the successful, I learned that "no often means that the acceptable time or option has not been discovered." Ray Kroc made eight trips to the bank before he got his loan for McDonald's.

Step #4   They have a strong and active faith in God or some higher power.

Businessman Charles Woods feels that in spite of his badly burned face and hands, he is one of the most blessed men. He, like others, finds a great deal of comfort in being able to call upon his Creator's help.

Ronald Reagan, President of the United States, says, "I have a deep-seated faith that if you ask for help, it will be given." He points to his mother, who left her legacy of faith with him.

Step #5   They are self disciplined, and decisive. They know what they want in life.

The successful were strategists. They had a main goal and a plan for obtaining it. If the first plan did not succeed, they had alternate strategies.

I have found six guidelines quite helpful in cultivating decisiveness. They are:

1. Weigh the pros and cons. Analyze the results. Ask yourself what is the worst thing that could happen. If you know the outer limits you will be less likely to fear a decision. Often we have a lot of imagined fears that inhibit us until we become concrete about them.

2. Write it out. Often, seeing the problem in black and white helps to focus it.

3. Then do it! Procrastination can be our way of avoiding responsibility.

4. Make decisions in areas that are worthy of your full attention. If you care and feel challenged by a decision, it will call into play the best of your abilities, and will therefore also maximize your chances for success.

5. Focus on the job at hand, is the advice of Philip Caldwell, Chairman of the Board, Ford Motor Company Retired, to those who want to get ahead: *"Whatever you are assigned to do, do it very well. Do the job at hand as well as you know how... don't spend all of your time on the present job trying to get to the next job... I think people hurt themselves, and they're not effective when they're doing that. You should be thinking very deeply about the job at hand, to do it better than anybody else. That is the biggest key that I know to open the next door."*

6. What if you make a mistake? Ray Kroc makes a good suggestion: *"When I make a*

> *mistake I throw it off by saying, that's why
> they put mats under cuspidors. You have to
> overcome your mistakes by making another
> decision. But I'd a heck of a lot rather people
> make mistakes than make nothing."*

Step #6   They enjoy their jobs even though some changed careers to achieve this satisfaction.

Florence Chadwick, record-breaking channel swimmer, changed stock-brokerage firms at age sixty when most people would have stayed for retirement benefits. Ray Kroc made it very clear: *"To love your work is very important. If you are going to prostitute yourself at an early age for dollars, you'll be working for dollars all your life."*

The creator of The Wizard of Oz, before his first success of the Oz story, couldn't seem to hold a job, failed to manage a hardware store, and had little respect shown to him in his own home. One day in middle age the Oz story came to him. His thoughts poured out after an electrical storm and he wrote most of the tale in 40 minutes. He went on after this first major success to produce over 250 entertaining programs in Hollywood, for which he was highly esteemed. He had failed to enjoy his other jobs until this child-like creativity emerged.

President Reagan reflected on entering politics: *"When they came to me and talked to me about running for Governor, I thought they were out of their minds. I had no desire to leave the life that I had. I said, I'll help you elect someone else. It was never really planned. And a couple of years after it happened, Nancy and I looked at each other one night and said, 'You know this makes everything else we've done as dull as dishwater.'"* "You didn't anticipate that?" I asked. "No," he said. "It was [satisfying] ...coping with the problems instead of just making speeches about them. Being able to do something about them was, I think, the most fulfilling thing of all."

Step #7   Have a sense of purpose in life and make a positive contribution to society.

Many of the successful felt they had a destiny. In most cases, our destiny is only gradually revealed to us, day by day. A few people have early visions that reveal a direction. Some people have dreams that point the way. Others follow a well thought out plan they have devised, to achieve a life-long objective.

The successful showed an inner strength, "a knowledge," that enabled them to move out of the ordinary at times when they felt the situation called for it. Not so much a rebellious act, it was the will to inspire a higher level of good in society. Maria Martinez, the most widely acclaimed native American potter was one such person. Though ostracized for it by the members of her tribe, she broke tradition by a tabooed sharing of the secret of making her pottery with women from other tribes. The new skills enabled these women to receive an income for their wares.

Charles Woods spoke of his brush with death in the fiery crash of his military plane, "It gave me a much more serious outlook on life and a feeling of wanting to help my fellow man."

The successful seemed to want to contribute to the society that had rewarded them generously in their professions. They expressed a deep appreciation of the opportunities America had provided them in the free enterprise system, and as a result, many were very patriotic.

The successful make every moment count. Charlton Heston admits to "overextending" himself; Malcolm Forbes "packs in" as much as he can every day. When I asked those interviewed in this book what they would do if they could do anything they wanted, most said they were already doing it. They weren't waiting until they retired to explore some new interest, they were already "packing it in."

They did not want to be frightened, as was the doctor in Katharine Anne Porter's Ship of Fools, who dreamed one night that he died, and cried out, "I can't be dead, I haven't lived."

Step #8 They are in good physical health, exercise regularly and discipline themselves in their eating habits.

Many of the successful engage in sports regularly. Charlton Heston and Norman Lear play in pro-celebrity tennis tournaments. Forrest Shumway, Vice Chairman of Allied-Signal Company often rides his bicycle to work. Artist Francoise Gilot does yoga, swims and has won horseback riding awards.

Step #9 They take time away from work to relax and renew themselves.

Most of the successful work hard and then they play hard. They shift their activities or pace and sometimes, their environment. Revitalizing themselves was crucial enough to actually schedule time for it.

Forrest Shumway resolutely makes time for his vacations; a week skiing with the family at Christmas, camping in the summer, and numerous hunting and fishing trips.

Summit Expedition Director Tim Hansel wrote the book, <u>When I Relax I Feel Guilty</u>, after an injury caused him to re-examine this aspect of his life. Anne Ruth, a quadriplegic, sparks up her routine by searching for new surroundings to enjoy with her family.

Malcolm Forbes travels through many countries on his motorcycle with a group of his colleagues and friends who get better acquainted with a wide range of citizens.

Step #10 Many were leaders since childhood.

World War II Ace General Jimmy Doolittle noticed

early in life that "the leaders were the boys with the ideas." He considered it more fun to create his own ideas than to follow the others. Norman Cousins, a boy of small physique and at the time in poor health, learned to become a leader without using the bullying tactics of the other boys by strengthening his techniques of negotiation.

Step #11 *They are androgynous.*

Many have androgynous traits that do not hinder them from doing things that are traditionally considered masculine or feminine. The successful know their strengths and weaknesses, which enables them to confidently express a strong self-assertiveness (as opposed to being aggressive). Florence Chadwick had always competed against boys in swimming, so it was easy for her to compete as a stock broker, in a predominantly male profession, without feeling threatened. Jill Ruckelshaus, U.S. delegate to the Women's International Year Conference, was actually surprised when she was not given the same opportunities as men in professional positions after graduating from college.

Sometimes the successful women did not look for discrimination and therefore didn't find it. When I asked Supreme Court Justice Sandra O'Connor how she had adjusted in a predominantly male profession she said, *"I don't think it has made much of a difference. I have found that people have been helpful and cordial to me throughout my career. I have discovered that if I worked hard and did a job well... I have been respected by both men and women.*

Step #12   They take risks.

Business executive Forrest Shumway made what others at the time might have considered daring changes in his company, and says that he is right in major decisions 75% of the time and thinks that is a good average. Ray Kroc defines "life's experiences" as "a compilation of all one's mistakes over the years." The bottom line is that it often takes many attempts to produce one success.

Summary

Success may sound simple but it requires more than mere luck to attain. It is important to be aware of your own special talents and interests. Ask yourself the question, "Why was I born?" What God given talents did you arrive with in this world? If your heart is set on a specific goal, career, or style of living, what will you be willing to sacrifice for your dream? Can you do it alone or do you want, or need, others? What will be the rewards and how will you know when you have attained success?

Will the journey be fun or will the fun only come with the end results? I believe that we are co-creators with our Maker. We need to do our part and develop our skills. But, we are not totally in charge of external circumstances, or even our own timing.

Can you be more successful than you are? Probably. I might add that the 12 Steps may seem simple. They are. If they are so simple, why have many people failed to attain their highest goals? There are a variety of reasons.

One common pitfall is that many people do not allow themselves to enjoy their "small" successes. They constantly sacrifice for the "one big break" which seems to keep eluding their grasp. They make discontentment a mental habit. If, as Norman Lear suggests, we collect our moments, then we are enjoying reaching for the goal as much or more so than we may enjoy the goal itself. If we are happy with our striving, then our failures are less frustrating and our success is an added delight.

It is common for successful people to direct their attention to other fulfilling pursuits, once they have attained their original goal. Bill Galt, founder of the Good Earth restaurant chain, after selling his business to General Mills, is rechanneling his energy and business know-how in a new direction. He said, "I used to spend 91% of my time working on my professional goals and 9% of my time helping with community and world projects. Now it is the reverse."

Life is an exciting challenge. The successful take the challenge and live every day to the fullest. *I wish the same for you!*

© 1987 Doris Lee McCoy

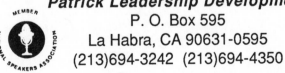

JOHN PATRICK DOLAN
Attorney -At-Large
Patrick Leadership Development
P. O. Box 595
La Habra, CA 90631-0595
(213)694-3242 (213)694-4350

John Patrick Dolan

John Patrick Dolan, Attorney At Large, is a hard charging trial attorney, a successful entrepreneur, and skilled motivator. You won't find a stronger advocate for personal growth, goal-oriented achievement and self realization. This self-made millionaire worked his way through college and law school with one of the most incredible employment histories imaginable. Jobs ranged from janitor for K-Mart, to Monorail driver at Disneyland, drummer for a rock and roll band, clothing salesman, insurance salesman, ticket seller and parking lot attendant for the California Angels, financial officer for a motion picture organization, and stock broker. Quite a laundry list! And, these jobs were before Dolan invested 10 years in developing his success in the courtroom as a trial attorney.

Dolan has been recognized as a nationally ranked College Debator, and a well prepared trial advocate. He speaks to both sides of the lawyer-client equation in the quest for creating balance and understanding. His lawyer audiences are genuinely interested in understanding and serving their clients. He explains the 5 Keys to building a successful practice of law.

His approach with business people is to identify important and relevant legal issues and then translate "legalese" to understandable English. Recent customized presentations on topics of current interest include: 1) *Employment is not a crime... yet, a Review of the Immigration Reform Act of 1986*; 2) *An oral contract is not worth the paper it's written on;* 3) *Power and Pitfalls of Small Claims Court;* 4) *How to be your lawyer's partner for fun and profit;* 5) *Report from Counsel.*

His Mission... helping lawyers serve their clients... helping YOU cope with Justice.

John Patrick Dolan, Attorney-At-Large, lives in La Habra Heights, California with his beautiful wife Irene and their daughter, Andrea Jennefer, "AJ."

Straight Talk From Your Attorney-At-Large

By John Patrick Dolan

*"The object contended for ought always
to bear some just proportion to the expense."*
        - Thomas Paine, "Common Sense"

Perry Mason

My Mom watched Perry Mason every day when I
was a child of impressionable years. I watched

too... a lot. This explains that while my name is quite Irish, my body tends to resemble my Mother's Italian heritage - and Raymond Burr. As Raymond Burr went from Perry Mason to Ironsides to "The Return of Perry Mason," I went from a size 39 to a size 44 coat. "Visual affirmations" are what my motivational-type friends call it. However, this is not why I am referred to as Attorney-At-Large.

Attorney-At-Large

Attorney-At-Large is another story. You see, as I progressed through my high school and college years I wore blinders. Your impressions and opinions about lawyars and what we represent mattered little to me. It wasn't easy but I knew what I wanted. Perry Mason the Second... a Criminal Trial Lawyer.

On my way through school I was simultaneously employed at one time or another as a stock broker, a drummer for a rock and roll band, a Monorail driver at Disneyland, a clothing salesman, a stereo salesman, an insurance salesman, a janitor for K-Mart, a ticket seller for the California Angels, a parking lot attendant for Anaheim Stadium and Convention Center, and the financial officer for a movie that would have been X-rated if we could have afforded to pay for the rating. All the while knowing my goal to practice criminal law was being progressively realized.

I did all this while married to my beautiful

wife, Irene. She stood by me all the while I was working several jobs and carrying a tremendous study load. I made it! I graduated. I opened my Law Offices, and then *you* pulled the rug out from under me!

You Hate Lawyers

After all my efforts to become Perry Mason's Second Coming, I discovered that you don't like lawyers. No, you virtually hate lawyers. Lawyers are nothing but money-grubbing, self-centered, unfeeling, uncaring, sleaze jerks. That's what you think, isn't it? Having an "Esq." behind my name was like a drunken sailor having a nifty tattoo applied... then waking up and finding out it cannot be removed without great effort and great pain.

I resolved that client by client, I would change your opinions. My services would be professional, sensitive, caring and reasonably priced. One by one you would be converted. There was one fatal flaw in my heartfelt approach. I am a <u>criminal</u> <u>lawyer</u>. Criminal lawyers handle cases for people charged with criminal offenses. Usually clients like their criminal lawyer... until they get acquitted or convicted. You see, if acquitted they didn't need me because the facts were obvious. If convicted I didn't do anything for them. This is what we call a win-win situation... right?

As my abilities improved and my talents sharpened, the local courts began to approach me to represent some <u>real</u> criminal types. Bad guys. The kind of folks that would kill and eat Bambi. My case load led me down the path that good, honest, intelligent, and well-meaning lawyers go down... my caseload created a condition called professional myopia. That is - nearsightedness compounded by hardening of the ego. I thought... you don't like lawyers? That's your problem! This was really conducive to good public relations!

A couple of years ago, having handled everything from parking tickets to death penalty murder cases, I decided to refocus my efforts toward helping you citizens understand my profession. I established my mission - to help lawyers serve their clients and to help YOU cope with justice. This mission statement was the genesis of Attorney-At-Large.

The Crime Problem

From a marketing point of view, criminal law has been a great place to spend my time as a lawyer. Crime is up and it appears unlikely that this "growth industry" will have a recession in the near future. However, you see the irony quite clearly. As my criminal practice grew and prospered, it was at the long term expense of our society. Don't get me wrong - I never encouraged crime - I just dealt with the mess once it was made.

The solution to the "crime problem" has been addressed in many ways. "Put <u>more</u> people in prison <u>longer</u> is one approach that is resulting in an overcrowded prison system. "Replace the judges" is a public favorite that is really popular these days - just ask former California Supreme Court Justice Rose Bird. There are many more - more police, less police, gun control, no gun control, K-9 Dog Patrols, security forces, alarm systems - and on and on.

It occurs to me as I'm sure it occurred to you, these so-called solutions <u>are not working</u>. Crime is booming.

The real truth is that crime is not an entity or product or a business or a phenomena unto its own - crimes are committed by people. People who commit crimes are by and large out of control. Their self control has left them either a little or a lot. A little, in the case of a minor misdemeanor or a non-fatal drunk driving case. A lot, in the case of a murder.

The people who commit these crimes are just like you and me, except for their periodic or continuous loss of control.

So, in my opinion, we need to focus on people <u>before</u> they get so out-of-control that they commit crimes. You and I are the answer to the crime problem. Each of us, one by one, needs to exercise the control over ourselves and our lives that makes crime an undesirable and unacceptable choice. We need to help others do the same. As our President, Ronald Reagan, has stated - "If not us... who? If not now... when?"

Everything You've Got

A famous criminal trial lawyer in Texas, Percy Foreman, tells a great lawyer's war story. Some years ago, a prospective client of Mr. Foreman's was accused of murder and faced the death penalty. The defendant visited the offices of the lawyer with the idea that an attorney-client relationship should be established and ultimately the charges beaten. The client explained in vivid but privileged detail the facts of the case and then got to the most important question. How Much? What would Mr. Foreman ask in attorney's fees if he decided to take the case? Foreman would take the case because Foreman was a good, honest, hard-working criminal lawyer. But, how much? The lawyer looked the client straight in the eye and said "everything you've got" is the fee.

The client was somewhat taken aback. Foreman had not asked the client anything about personal finances, family support, any form of assets. The client asked, as surely most would, "What do you mean?" "Son, said the old Texan, "You're charged with the death penalty... understand?" The client nodded understandingly. "And son, you want me to do everything I can to win your case and save your life... right?" Again the client nodded. "Well then, Son, your fee will be everything you've got. Because, if I win I will be worth it... and if I lose you won't need it anyway!"

The price for our society to solve the "crime problem" is the same - everything we've got. Not by taxing ourselves into oblivion, not be spending every last dime on law enforcement. The price is paradoxical. It won't cost a penny and yet it's everything we've got. Each of us needs to solve our own crime problem. Each of us needs to control our conduct so as to make crime an unacceptable alternative for ourselves.

In saying this I realize that there are limited numbers of mental defectives who cannot or will not control themselves. We must protect and defend ourselves from the psychopath. However, I am reminded of the famous fractured phrase, "We have met the enemy - and he is us."

Justice, the Law and Your Lawyers

Justice is the goal - the intended destination - the optimum. Our legal institutions from the Supreme Court of the United States, to the Federal Circuit Court of Appeals, to the Federal District Trial Courts... from your State Supreme Court to your Justice or Small Claims Court... in and about every one of our legal institutions we seek the concept of justice. We seek fairness, personal responsibility, and individual freedom.

The law is the tool box of instruments that are used to make justice happen. Just as a mechanic would only use the tools that are necessary for a particular job - certain laws are the tools we use for particular legal matters. But, just like Mr. Goodwrench, lawyers need to know what their tool box should contain and the types of repair work they will be called upon to perform.

Your lawyers are the mechanics. Lawyers apply the law to your repair problems in the quest for justice. Divorce, child custody, personal injury, property damage, contracts and all manner of claims and counter claims are "worked on" by lawyers every day.

I perceive that you view justice, the law, and your lawyers as the good, the bad, and the ugly. Your lawyers are good hardworking people who deserve better. But you deserve better too. We owe you better service, communication, and explanation. I want to assist you and your cause.

Lawyers, Clients and Other Strange Bedfellows

As I've traveled around the country speaking to lawyer's groups about how to better serve their clients, and business groups about how to deal with lawyers, the law, and justice, something interesting has emerged. The same things lawyers need to do to be successful in their professional capacity are the things you need to do to be successful in your life. I venture to make the incredible statement that lawyers and real people have th same or very similar kinds of lives. All of us have professional, family, social, mental, physical, and spiritual lives. If we balance our lives among these competing interests we can enjoy the God-given gifts we possess.

If all the lawyers in America would seek to obtain a balance in their lives and if all clients would do the same, then we could go a long way toward solutions. Solutions to the crime problem and solutions to some of the other legal messes we get ourselves into - divorce, contract breach, injury caused to others, business problems and so on. If we get ourselves right first then we may find it easier to deal with others.

The primary presentation I make to lawyer's groups is called the 5 Keys to the Successful Practice of Law. This program was developed over the years by observing what the really good lawyers did to be really good lawyers. Not law library research efforts, although such work is absolutely necessary to proper preparation. I mean, how did the really successful lawyers conduct themselves generally and then in relation to their clients.

Over time I have come to realize that the 5 Keys are not limited to lawyers. Anyone can use these concepts to live a richer, more productive and fulfilling life. See if you agree.

Key Number 1 - Building Client Loyalty

We lawyers call the users of our services "Clients." In other professions or industries they are called patients, customers, buyers, and consumers. You are called a client by your lawyer, a patient by your doctor, a buyer by your salespersons, and a consumer by your utility providers (and possibly David

Horowitz). The same YOU is all of those.

Keeping our clients is a full time occupation. Clients need to feel important. You want someone to believe in, something to believe in and someone to believe in you.

Something to believe in... people need to believe in the product they consume. I can tell you this is so having seen people in their greatest time of need. People want to believe the Justice System works.

Someone to believe in... you've heard it many times: You buy the salesman as much or more than you buy his product. In my profession it's an everyday occurrence. My clients want me, not my associates.

Someone to believe in you... Here is the real central idea in building relations with others. Nothing substitutes for the good feelings you get when you truly believe someone believes in you.

If we will keep our focus on our clients, their needs, their understanding, their feelings, then we will develop the loyalty that makes for lasting, fulfilling, profitable relationships.

Key Number 2 - Building a Public Image

You never get a second chance to make a good first impression. And you know first impressions are the most lasting.

How you are perceived by your client, potential clients, and the community at large can make a substantial difference in both income and mental wages.

Think of the person you would like to become and then constantly ask yourself "How would that person conduct himself?" Acting "as-if" you are that person in every instance will eventually cause you to become that person.

Key Number 3 - Developing Greater Productivity

Everyone begins every day with the same amount of time. Yet, some get more done than others. My study of the most productive lawyers and other professionals has shown me at least part of the reason why.

The most productive people "major on the majors." They know that being <u>efficient</u> is not nearly so important as being <u>effective</u>. Efficiency is doing things right. Effective is doing the right things.

You must identify the five or six activities in your business (and life for that matter) and consistently, habitually direct your efforts toward those priorities. You will get more done in less time.

Key Number 4 - Creating Clear Thinking and Increased Energy

Dale Carnegie used to tell the story of The Two Woodsmen who spent a day chopping wood. One woodsman chopped and chopped from sunup to sundown. The other woodsman chopped for a while then sat and rested for a while, chopped and rested, chopped and rested.

By the end of the day the woodsman who had been working without stopping all day was dismayed to observe that the other woodsman had cut three times as much wood. "How could this be?" he asked. "Well, you see," replied his associate, "Each time I sat down to rest I took time to sharpen my axe!"

We must sharpen our mental and physical axes a little each day. Good vigorous aerobic exercise is vital to clear thinking and increased energy. Play a game of racquetball or ride a bike or go to the local aerobics class. The benefits to you compounded with consistent exercise... and you'll be sharpening your "axe."

Key Number 5 - Planning Your Future

The one thing that separates the super achievers from the rest of humanity is a written and specific plan of action for your business and personal life. We are self directing, self correcting beings and if we chart a clear course our distination is virtually guaranteed.

The "slight edge" concept applies here. A .250 hitting baseball player makes a handsome salary. A .333 hitter makes literally millions well over ten times his .250 hitting counterpart. The difference in hitting in 3 games is this:

				Total
At Bats:	4	4	4	12
.250 Hitter	1	1	1	3
.333 Hitter	1	1	2	4

Just one more hit in twelve at bats gains a return that is tenfold greater. So it is with our lives and our accomplishments. A written and specific goal program gets us a tenfold return in business and personal life. Why not be a big hitter? The choice is yours.

The Final Argument

I speak to both sides of the lawyer-client equation in the quest for creating balance and understanding. My lawyer audiences are genuinely interested in understanding and serving their clients. I explain to them the 5 Keys to building the successful practice of law. The improvement in performance and attitude is dramatic. And you, my friend, are the beneficiary.

My approach with you business people is to identify legal issues that are important and relevant to you and then translate "legalese" to understandable English. Examples of recent topics are: 1) <u>Employment is not a crime... yet, a Review of the Immigration Reform Act of 1986</u>; 2) <u>An oral contract is not worth the paper it's written on</u>; 3) <u>Power and Pitfalls of Small Claims Court</u>; 4) <u>How to be your lawyer's partner for fun and profit</u>; and, 5) <u>Report from Counsel</u>. These are customized presentations on topics of current interest to business and industry. By meeting outside the traditional law office setting, face to face, we can break down barriers between lawyer and client.

In addition, whenever I speak to a non-lawyer audience, I collect from you a survery which includes your feeling on justice, and your lawyer. This provides a continuing data base and feedback system for my colleagues. I can literally tell my attorney friends what you are presently feeling about our professional performance with very little time lapse.

The combination of my presentations to and between attorney audiences and lay organizations and companies is how I implement my mission of **Attorney-At-Large.**

The world is before you, and you need not take it or leave it as it was when you came in.
                                        - James Baldwin

PETER SUMNER
15 The Grove
Camberwell Vic 3124
AUSTRALIA
(03)299-2085   (03)299-4994

Peter Sumner

Peter grew up in Melbourne and was training at a teacher's college when he lost his sight through an accident. He taught for several years with the Braille and Talking Book Library of Victoria, and in 1969 became the National Director of the Christian Blind Mission International (Australia), a service organisation which assists handicapped people through "Love in Action" projects all over the world.

Peter was a founding Board member of "Foresight," the Australian Overseas Aid and Prevention of Blindness organisation, and helped to establish the National Federation of Blind Citizens of Australia and the Melbourne radio station for the print-handicapped. He was the first blind executive to be trained at the Australian Administrative Staff College. He is an Associate Member of the Australian Institute of Management and a member of the National Speakers Association of Australia.

Peter is well-known for his descriptive writing. His first book, "Here Comes Trouble," was published in 1980. His wife pearl is partially blind and the Director of CBMI's Library Services for the Print-Handicapped. She is a talented singer. Peter and Pearl have traveled widely in connection with their work.

The Sumners have two children (fully sighted) and the family lives in Camberwell, a suburb of Melbourne. At home, Peter enjoys books, gardening, and jogging with Luther, his golden labrador guide-dog.

Trouble is What You Climb On

By Peter Sumner

"A man climbs because he needs to climb, because that is the way he is made. Rock and ice and wind and the great blue canopy of the sky are not all that he finds upon the mountain-tops. He discovers things about his own body and nind that he had almost forgotten in the day-to-day, year-to-year routine of living. He learns what his legs are for, what his lungs are for, what the wise men of old meant by 'refreshment of the spirit"

JamesRamseyUllman

The idea of going on an adventure holiday occurred to me one evening while travelling home from the office on the tram.

"My son David will be seventeen by Christmas," I thought. "Just the age to enjoy a bit of bushwalking and camping out. Next year, when he turns eighteen, he will probably get a car and want to spend the holidays careering from beach to beach with his mates.

This is the time. An opportunity I shouldn't miss. "The experience would be good for us both. The only question... where to go?"

In January, Queensland Australia is prone to tropical storms and cyclones, so I decided the direction to go was south. Next day I rang the Tasmanian Tourist Bureau. (Tasbureau) Soon I received information about "adventures" to be enjoyed on the Holiday Isle. One company I shall call "Wilderness Walks" advertised a seven day trek along the coastline of the southwest cape. It began from Hobart and was entitled something like "Away N Trek Wild." Sounded just the thing. I applied for two reservations.

Tasbureau confirmed our bookings. I thought, "should I mention my special situation to them? There had been no provision in their application forms for it. I had lost my sight at nineteen through an accident with raw lime (whitewash) while on a working bee with some college friends.

After a period of adjustment I had come to think of myself as being visually inconvenienced, rather than visually impaired. I wrote to Tasbureau: "I am a perceptually challenged person. I have had to learn how to live, work and achieve effectively using my four senses of touch, taste, smell and especially hearing, which I have developed to an extraodinary degree. I am quite fit, usually jogging several kilometers each morning. I have traveled widely around the world, often in rugged "out-of-the-way" places, have climbed a mountain in America, and crawled down lava holes to underground caverns in Japan."

The manager of Melbourne Tasbureau indicated "Wilderness "Walks" would be in touch with me. The operator, whom I shall call "Bill Graves," called to say he would come to Melbourne to discuss my participation. Mr. Graves told me almost immediately he had misgivings about my ability to cope in a wilderness enviroment, even with a guide. He described the rough conditions.

I did my best to explain how David and I could manage. Finally he appeared satisfied.

A Handle On The Expedition

All systems were "go." I began preparations. First, the wilderness equipment. David and I bought boots, gaiters, pants, shirts, odds and ends. Then I got a Blackhall handle. This rectangular guiding apparatus, about 44cm long and 13cm wide is named for the well-known English blind mountain climber, poet and broadcaster, David Scott Blackhall.

Blackhall visited Australia and stayed in our home where he showed me the guiding handle he designed and used for climbing Mount Snowdon. It is like the handle on a guide-dog harness, except it has a handgrip at both ends, one for the guide, one for the blind person. You can't buy these. I had to have a high-tensile aluminium one made up.

What about physical fitness? As a balance to the sedentary nature of my work I had begun a programme of long early morning walks with my guide dog, "Luther," a big strong male golden labrador. But walking didn't give me all the excercise I wanted in the time available, so I tried jogging. To my delight Luther could guide me just as effectively at this faster pace, providing we both knew the route well and jogged in the quiet of early morning. We ran in short bursts along familiar footpaths near our Camberwell home.

I decided I would add the same distance again in the evening, wearing the boots I planned to take to Tasmania. Covering nine kilometres daily during the months prior to the winderness trek would enable me to cope with the expedition rigours. I didn't realize that the rigours would not be the small kind, but those with a big capital **R,** underlined!

Difficult Path

At first, arrangements seemed normal. I had sent Tasbureau a cheque to cover the full cost of our adventure holiday. The Manager, Mr. Chaperon, sent a cordial note with my receipt, "We hope you both have a thoroughly enjoyable time down there."

I rang Mr. Graves at his home to check our "What To Bring" list. To my surprise he again expressed anxiety about my participation in his tour. He soon seemed reassured, and gave me names and particulars about our fellow walkers.

Fateful Irony

Mr. Grave's letter cancelling our reservations was recieved and read to me by David on 13 December, the anniversary of the accident that had caused the loss of my sight.

Mr. Graves had had a change of heart. The only reason he gave was that he was no longer prepared to accept the risks involved in my participation. He concluded with a curt offer to pay any extra costs incurred by me.

How do you put a price on the hurt, humiliation and disappointment of such rejection? When I rang Mr. Graves I could only get onto his answering machine. He was away on another walking tour. With barely two weeks to go before departure I wrote a desperate letter pleading for his reconsideration.

"David and I are ready to undertake any fair test you may arrange," I said. "We can prove we can cope with very rough walking conditions. We will be happy to abide by the assessment of an impartial judge if you would give it, and us, a go."

Mr. Graves finally phoned one evening. He could not be persuaded and stood doggedly by his decision. When I asked why, he said he could not see how I would be able to cope with bushes against my face, makeshift toilet arrangements, and steep climbs.

The Real Viewpoint

It was useless to pursue it. I had to face the fact that given any situation in life, especially where a handicapped person is concerned: **Some people only see problems, while others see possibilities.**

I felt hung in suspension. Had I attempted too much? Was I presumptuous to think David and I could take part in an advertised adventure holiday like any other father and son? I was tempted to give up, but that meant moral capitulation. I was not prepared to let someone else decide without a fair assessment what I could or could not achieve. No one can set the limits and boundaries of my experience. So I determined that David and I would have a bush-walking holiday in Tasmania. The challenge itself was an adventure.

I contacted Mr. Chaperon at Tasbureau. He was shocked by Mr. Graves' abrupt last minute decision, but could not force him to change his mind. I asked if they could find an adventure holiday operator who would be willing to take us on a tour in the next few weeks.

Mr. Chaperon called back to say that Mr. Eric Sargent, owner/manager of Craclair Tours had a couple of openings for his 7 day Cradle Mountain National Park tour December 28, and would be happy to take us! The arrangements were rushed through just before Christmas.

Opportunity: The Real Treasure

Eric Sargent, in his early sixties, has conducted tours for clients through the wild beauty of north central Tasmania for twenty years. He was one of the first to recognize its potential for tourism. He told me in his slow, almost deliberate drawl that his ambition was to create an opportunity for all Australians to have access to the magnificent wilderness of our national heritage. A thorough professional and true Australian adventurer, Eric will give anything a "go" if he believes some good will come of it. He had arranged cabin-based trips recently in the wilderness for sixteen handicapped people and their enablers. They all had a wonderful time.

The Great Adventure Begins

The early flight took us to the picturesque little city of Devonport on a clear bright morning. We were transported to a local scout hall used by Eric Sargent for his clients and guides.

Eric's cheery welcome put us at ease straight away. Since the tour did not start 'till afternoon, he suggested a walk about town. We set out at a brisk pace along the foreshore to the lighthouse bluff, clambering over a rocky promontory. We sat in the warm sunshine and listened to the lapping sounds of a gentle sea. We lunched on the biggest, tastiest, most delightfully cooked scallops at the Tamahere Hotel, and at half the price we would pay on the mainland.

Our Mates

From Melbourne there were two nurses, a plumber and his wife, newlylweds, a married couple who were teachers. From Sydney a professional potter, a solicitor, his wife, daughter and son. Also an older couple who spoke to each other in Hungarian, and, recovering from jetlag, a young male nurse from Seattle Washington.

Eric called us together to meet the guides. Neil, a devoted, experienced bushwalker in his thirties. Lise, a young woman of extraodinary cheerful vitality. Dico, strong, stolid and patient. Cadet assistants were Warren and Jesse, both about 20. Each carried large packs with all of their own gear plus cooking utensils and first aid kits. They would set up camp, provide meals and ensure the well-being of the walkers. Our own equipment was a rucksack, semi-inflatible mattress, sleeping bag, waterproofs and eating utensils. Adding our own things, our packs weighed about 12 kilos. We were each handed a whistle on a lanyard to blow if we got separated. I took a mini-cassette recorder on which to make notes, and of course my Blackhall handle.

Our driver, Dennis Maxwell, was loud, boisterous and fun loving. His extensive, intimate knowledge of the area and dare-devil driving on narrow winding roads was safe but never dull. The thin branches whipped at our windows, we careened around bends, swooped into hollows and roared up steep inclines while he laughed and shouted to us. He delivered us and our gear to Waldheim, the National Park northern entrance. A small Rufus wallaby hopped out of the bushes nearby. David led me slowly over to where it was nibbling, unafraid of people. We both stroked its long ears and silky fur.

Enabling Techniques

Our guiding technique was simple. Where the ground was not too rough, David held the front grip of the Blackhall, I the back one, like the connecting rod between the wheels of a steam train. When David wanted both hands free he strapped his end to his rucksack. For very rough or steep terrain, I moved up closer and with my free hand lightly gripped the back of his rucksack. On the steepest slopes we used the handle to pull or lower me.

We set off in single file through a marshy area over a wooden walkway made of slats. Not too bad, but all too soon the walkway finished. We toiled upward on a muddy trenchlike track through the scrub. It became rockier as it took us through a wooded area beside a fast-flowing stream.

The first waterfalls were Crater Falls over-arched by tall trees catching and holding the descending symphony of cascading water. Rocks and low tree trunks were clad in thick moist iridescent green moss. The cool air had a rich earthy frangrance. We climbed on and up through timber and scrub until we came to Crater Lake, brooding in eerie stillness. The guides handed 'round cups of fruit saline and jelly beans, a welcome feature of all our rest stops.

A steep climb over rocky ground brought us to Marion's Lookout, a panoramic view. As the sun's rays through the clean clear air made themselves felt, we applied sunblock to noses, necks and arms. We tramped over tracts of loose stones, mud, wirey alpine vegetation and came to a shel-tered hollow near running water where we had lunch. Dry biscuits with spreads, nuts, raisins, cheese and cold sausage were washed down by tea or coffee. Then we began the real challenge, the ascent of Cradle Mountain.

We took off our rucksacks and stuffed indis-pensable japara waterproof jackets into the small nylon backpacks we had been given, leaving our other things in the shelter of some scrub. My feet slipped on the steep incline. As we encountered bigger boulders, David leaped to the top with youthful strength and agility, planted his feet firmly, and hauled me up with the handle. I hardly had time to catch my breath before he was on the next one, ready to haul again.

This Is Your Mountain

I was wet with perspiration, gasping for breath. It was far more demanding than I had anticipated. Then I remembered something David Scott Blackhall had written. It had helped me face the loss of my sight.

"Climbing a mountain is an epitome of life. When you are half way up, it's no use wishing you had come another day, or tackled it from the other side, or climbed a different mountain altogether. This is the mountain you must climb. The one which is under your feet."

The tumbled pile of huge boulders became even more precipitous. It was impossible for David to lead and haul me. I had to use my hands as well as my feet, relying on directions shouted from my fellow climbers. Aware of what could happen if I slipped and fell, I felt relaxed and confident. I knew I had plenty of time to place my hands and feet carefully, and to check my balance before each move. I felt sorry for those around me who could see, because surely they could not be enjoying it as much as I.

My spirit soared into the broad blue sky as I climbed the last few hundred metres to the top of Cradle Mountain. We came to a minor peak, then the major one through a "cradle-like" hollow.

Snow here was granulated as if made up of small hail. I ate a few handfuls to quench my thirst. A free-for-all snow fight broke out with much shouting and laughter. David bumped me over and dragged me down the entire length of the drift leaving me drenched and almost frozen. But I was soon warmed by the short, arduous climb to the top. A strange quietness settled upon the group as they surveyed the magnificence. We munched jelly beans and rested. Suddenly I realized the tips of my fingers and heels of my palms were sore and lacerated with scores of tiny cuts. During the next fortnight or so I was to find it hard to read braille or use my braille watch. "Next time, I'll bring gloves!"

My thoughts went back to an August day in New Hampshire, U.S.A., climbing Mount Monadnock with my blind friend Graham Laycock. The guide had said **"The rough places afford the best footholds. They are what we use to get to the top."**

Handicap of Champions

Every horse that starts in the famous Melbourne Cup is handicapped. Yet each horse has a chance of winning. Blindness, I realised, did not disqualify me from the race of life. It makes it a bit harder to achieve, but not impossible.

To reach the top of any mountain in life, we must adopt and maintain positive mental attitudes. Psychologists recognise development of healthy self-image is fundamental for personal happiness and success. That is why I choose to regard myself as being handicapped, rather than disabled. "Disabled" signifies something or someone broken down, ceasing to function effectively, and broken. A handicap is merely an encumbrance or disadvantage that you have to take into account as you strive for your goal.

I decided to adopt a positive attitude and to become a possibility thinker. After a great deal of experience in my work with handicapped people over the past twenty years, I am firmly convinced: **A person with four senses and a positive attitude will achieve far more than a person with five senses and a negative one.**

Moment Of Embarrassment

Our descent from Cradle Mountain was a greater strain than the climb up. It would have been too slow if I had clambered down backwards, facing the up-slope. I had to turn around and slide forward, stepping or jumping from one boulder to the next, guided by David's instructions. As David preceeded me going down, his head would often be below my knees, with nothing to hold on to. I fought back the feeling that any lack of attention by either of us would have me pitch headlong into the void. Once we reached the lower slopes, I took the handle again. When we reached the rucksacks I discovered to my embarrassment that the seat of my new pants had been torn to shreds by the sliding descent.

Lise offered to guide me the final 2 and 1/2 hour trek to our campsite. I was extremely tired, and hardly had the strengh to talk to her. It was nine p.m. We had begun at 8:30 that morning. Dinner was served beside a scenic lake. Reconstituted chicken, stewed apple, custard. "Hunger makes good sauce." For me, each campsite beside scenic lakes, rivers and waterfalls had its own distinctive sounds, smells, textures. That first night I learned to wash myself without letting my soap pollute the icy cold stream, while perched precariously on a small rock at the water's edge.

We stood in a horse-shoe around the smoking campfire enjoying conversation, while holding our socks out to dry draped over sticks, before we tucked into our two-man pup tent.

What Makes The Difference?

Of all the beautiful trees, the ones that made the greatest impression on me were those wonderful sentinals, the pencil pines. We lunched one day sheltered by a magnificent specimen our guides estimated to be possibly fifteen hundred years old. I felt its surface roots, laid my cheek against the silky fibrous bark and touched its delicate needles. I thought of all the empires, governments and people it had outlived. I was awed by this solitary tree, now threatened by big business and the chain-saw.

No less memorable, the wicked scaparia bushes tore at our clothes and scratched us with hard prickly leaves.

Button-grass, with its tough ribbon-like grass supporting small, button-like seed pods can help or hinder a wilderness traveler. It springs from a thick unyielding base which can easily trip the unwary hiker. But in boggy places it often provides a firm footing amid treacherous mud and ooze.

A wise person once said, '**THE ONLY DIFFERENCE BETWEEN STUMBLING BLOCKS AND STEPPING STONES IS THE WAY WE USE THEM.**'

Adventure All Around

Equally fascinating were the many forms of wildlife which our mates described to me as we went along. Bennetts and Rufus wallabies, and their diminutive cousins, the potoroos. Several echidnas, (a small, spiny insect-eating mammal), the sleepy wombat, (a large, burrowing marsupial), and a glistening black snake that quickly glided off the track.

Many birds inhabited the forests and thickets lower down the slopes. They would often sport bright colors and chirp enquiringly at us from twigs barely an arms length away.

Near the top of Mount Ossa, a rare variety of freshwater shrimp was noticed in a small pool. When we stopped for lunch at Lake Wills, I inadvertently sat on a nest of jumping ants and was galvanized into frantic activity by their firey bites.

At Pelion Hut campsite small loathsome leathery-like leeches infested the whole area. These repulsive predators leaped with amazing agility onto our boots and crawled up our pants legs. If still moving they could be flicked off, but once they had begun feeding the only safe way to remove them is to touch them with the hot head of a match that has just been extinguished. We took refuge in our tents, killing the leeches that came in with us and zipping up the entrance. When the sun went down, the frenzied efforts of these parasites all but ceased.

Nature's Power

In one week we encountered heavy rain, bubbling springs, shaded forest pools, broad lakes, swamps, snow drifts, rushing streams, placid rivers and most delightful of all, roaring waterfalls. I will never forget the steep descent from Du Cane Hut into the gorge where Cathedral, D'Alton and Fergusson Falls drop their long white bridal veils in thundering torrents over dark cliffs and jutting rocks edged with emerald green moss. The sound of the falls suggest power and force.

My runs at home had done little to prepare my feet for the ruggged Tasmania conditions. Like most blind people I kick the toes of my shoes against steps & curbs. I must have kicked my boots against most of the roots, rocks and boulders on the trail. When I took off my boots I found blisters under my big toes. One of the guides taped my toes with elastoplast and loaned me a thin pair of cotton socks to wear inside my thicker woolen ones, which made a big difference.

The brisk pace made my response to the Blackhall handle like a reflex. I had to move immediately when it did, without hesitation. First I tried to visualize what the ground would be like. The effort left me wet with perspiration, especially since I have a weak ankle which turned suddenly several times. I feared the inability to walk.

Then I remembered a book entitled "The Inner Game of Tennis," by Timothy Gallwey. He says, **success comes more readily when we make less conscious effort, and allow the body to feel its way into the game.**

I stopped thinking for my feet, and started thinking with them. I focused on other things, and allowed my feet to feel their way. Not easy at first, but I found I was more relaxed and better able to cope with hazards.

Despite David's efforts, the rugged terrain did defeat us occasionally. I slipped and fell more than most. I rememberd an Austrailan author, Alan Marshall, who was handicapped by childhood polio. He wrote in his book, "These Are My People": **"Falls to those who walk on crutches in rough places, are a common place. You take them in your stride. I exploited my falls by extending the period in which I lay on the ground so that I**

could examine ants and tiny insects - all the
things that can only be enjoyed when your face
is just above the earth. Only people who fall
know of the world beneath a blade of grass."

So when I fell I examined the rocks. I crushed
leaves in my fingers, discovering a sweet or astrin-
gent fragrance to share with the others.

But what of the views, the things I could not
share? It was Lise who rapturously described the
stars to me the morning after New Year's Eve. I
found myself enjoying her joy. Various members of
our party described to me, each in their own way,
what they saw. These pleasures were enjoyed
vicariously, **but enjoyed nevertheless.**

All This And Heaven Too

When we share, our joys are heightened, our
sufferings diminished. As if the beauties of nature
poured out around us in wild extravagant abundance on our trek were not enough, I discovered
several others in our party, who, like me, greatly
loved books and writing. Warren took turns in
guiding me while we discussed our favorite authors.

Once as we passed a thicket we heard the
unusual cry of a bushbird. Warren mimicked it. To
our delight the bird answered, and answered me
too, fluttering from branch to branch to keep up
with us.

Journey's End

We came at last to the little suspension bridge over the Narcissus River. Our journey's end. We walked along a series of planks suspended by rods from steel cables on either side which served as handrails just below shoulder level. The bridge bounced rythmically as I dragged my weary feet across and climbed down the ladder. For me, the trek had been totally demanding of mind and body. I was exhausted.

When we got to the cabin for the final night, who should be there to greet us but our loud, ebullient driver, Dennis Maxwell. "Well, yuz got here at last!" he roared in mock surprise. I don't think I have ever heard a more welcome speech than his. After showers that revived our grimy bodies and weary spirits, the guides served a hearty meal of soup, stew and fruit salad. We toasted our guides with champagne.

What Is Life?

Next day, Eric Sargent was waiting for us when we pulled up at the scout hall. My son David turned to me with a grin over another meal of those wonderful scallops, and said, "Well Dad, we did it. Are you happy?"

"Yes son, I'm very happy." I turned to Eric and asked, "Do you know if any other blind person has ever climbed Cradle Mountain or walked through the national park?"

"I think," he said slowy, "you are probably the first."

One thing I know, I won't be the last "perceptually challenged" person to do it.

The trip demonstrated the value of team work. It was one of the hardest things I had ever done, but it gave a great deal more than it took. When handicapped people are given the opportunity to show what they can do, they can triumph.

My brief encounter with the wilderness and all that led up to it reminded me that if we want peak experiences, we will have to climb mountains; that if we want victories, we cannot avoid battles; and that if we want achievements, we must persevere in our pursuit of worthwhile goals.

I thought of what Hellen Keller said when she was initally barred from entering Radcliffe College simply because she was deaf and blind: **"Avoiding danger is no safer in the long run than outright exposure. Life is either a daring adventure...or nothing."**

STEVEN HALPERN
Sound Rx
P.O. Box 2644
San Anselmo, CA 94960
(415)485-5321

Steven Halpern

When people speak of relaxing and soothing music, the first name that comes to mind is Steven Halpern. He has helped transform the field of modern music by establishing the scientific, medical and economic viability of what is commonly called "New Age Music."

But Steven is much more than just a composer and recording artist. He is a highly vocal advocate of "Sound Health," and maintains an active schedule of speaking engagements and media appearances.

"Your body is literally a 'human instrument,'" he points out, "and the better you learn how to keep it in tune, the better you'll work, play, and enjoy life in general."

A modern Renaissance man, Steven Halpern is a successful entrepreneur, the president and CEO of his own internationally-distributed record label, and a consultant to corporations and health organizations of all kinds.

As he relates in the following chapter, he didn't wake up one morning and decide to change the music industry or the educational institutions where he did his under-graduate and graduate work. But being a Mover, Shaker and Change Agent has always come naturally to him. To paraphrase a famous advertising paradigm, "He sees a need and acts on it." He shares some of his successes, techniques, and suggestions for how you can tap into your own inner resources to support and enhance the Mover and Shaker within You.

Moving and Shaking to Your Own Inner Rhythm

By Steven Halpern

What a joy it is to be able to serve others as we serve ourselves."   -Ram Dass

I learned at an early age that I had a choice when things in my life weren't as I liked — or needed. I could be a victim of chance and "fate," passively reacting to events and situations — or I could take an active role in designing and creating my own reality. In other words, acting rather than re-acting.

Given the choice I'd much rather be in charge of my reality than allow someone else to decide for me. After all, it seemed only natural that I would know more accurately what was right for me than someone else.

Throughout my life, I have found that if I paid attention to the "inner voice" (that we all have) and stayed true to its calling, my life would work better. I'd be happier, healthier, more productive and creative than when I didn't follow what felt right to me.

Years later, I found out that such a philosophy of life also helped make me "a mover and shaker" even if I wasn't aware of it at the onset. Many times, however, when the external world did not fit my vision of what "should be," I'd find myself "rushing in where angels fear to tread." I might often be winging it, flying by the seat of my pants... but most always landing on my feet.

In the process, I wound up getting the opportunity to make a difference, and to contribute meaningfully to the betterment of my fellow men and women.

Shake Up the Status Quo

In my life, three successes stand out as having moved the most energy and shaken up the status quo the most. Each began innocently enough. The first took place in the hallowed halls of academia: the others in the "outside world."

When I was an undergraduae at the University of Buffalo the School motto upheld the right of each student to self-actualize. I took the folks at their word. All I did was humbly suggest that my need to self-actualize did not include taking six credit hours of statistics and calculus, and DID include taking numerous courses outside of my declared major. It also meant taking some classes that weren't offered, which I was fully prepared to develop and administer myself. (I KNEW, even then, that I could hire someone to do that work for me, if and when I ever needed it, and much more cost effectively than I could do it myself. Yes, that was one of the few times it would be better to have someone else do it if you wanted it done right).

Long before I read about it in any educational journal, I knew that I learned best that which I was most motivated to learn. At that point in my life, what really grabbed my attention was an insatiable curiosity about the philosophies of different cultures. I wanted to know what each had to say about our purpose in living on this planet.

I found incredible joy and fulfillment in reading the works of Plato, Aristotle, Confucius, Krishnamurti, Gurdjieff, and William Blake. I wasn't concerned that such studies did not seem to have an immediate practical application. Not did I know then that they would all be useful, in a very coherent,synoptic way years later. Indeed, I had no ulterior motive, other than that I wanted to do it, then and there. It felt good, it felt right, right down to the core of my being.

There was one little problem with this scenario, however. The university system allowed a student to take one 4-credit elective in the areas that I elected to take 40 credits worth!

"If You Don't Like the News, Make Some of Your Own"
or
"Everybody's Talking About the Weather, But..."

I was fortunate to have as one of my mentors a philosophy instructor named Jeremy Taylor, who suggested that if I didn't like the status quo, I could change it.

Voila! That hadn't occurred to me. I was raised in the "grumble and complain" school of thought. But how could I take on such a monolithic adversary as the University, which, at 30,000 strong, was really a universe-city.

I asked Jeremy how to begin, and was reminded that "In Unity there is Strength." Indeed, our very country is founded on that principle. "Go out, make some speeches and write some articles for the school paper. There are probably lots of others like you who feel the same way, but are too timid to speak up. Chances are they'll rally behind you. Then you can sign a petition, and present your request to the Dean's office. They're much more likely to pay attention to many voices than to one."

I walked out of Jeremy's office, ready to take on the system... and realized I had never made a speech in front of people. Sure, there were those times in English class when we all had to give a book report to what amounted to a captive audience.

Now, I not only would have to speak to an audience who may or may not be my peers, but I had to finagle a way to get them to hear me out in the first place.

That opportunity provided me with the incentive to study with people like Mario Savio, Paul Goodman, Edgar Z. Friedenberg, and John Holt, the ideological patron saints of progressive education.

I had jumped in— it was sink or swim. Given the alternative of acting like a fool in front of a room full of empty seats, I set out to learn "how to do it."

My trial by fire got me into theatrics, and I learned the positive power of enthusiasm in getting my message across to an audience. This, of course, is something that most all good public speakers know. It's the same thing the preacher knows, and uses, on Sunday morning to motivate his congregation.

In sum, I recognized the nature of the challenge, and did what was necessary to get the job done. I assembled the tools, employed the techniques, and went about putting forth my vision of how it ought to be.

Now, I won't tell you that the entire platform of requests of our All-Academic Union were accepted immediately by the University. But I will tell you that I was the first student to graduate with 40 units of electives in the history of the school!

Not only that, the following year, an entire new division opened up as part of the Experimental College that encouraged students to design their own curricula. To this day, that opportunity is available to students who want — and need— it.

My name may not be permanently engraved on the marble columns for all to see, but the change remains. I know that this transformation didn't happen by itself — and I have the clippings to prove who did the MOVING AND SHAKING.

A Serendipitous Sabbatical

While I was an undergraduate, my role models and heroes were the graduate students and professors. My goal was to become like them, and continue in their footsteps, helping to turn undergraduates on to the wonderful world of self-actualization, and of becoming who and what they really are.

That was not in the stars, however. The year I graduated was also the year that huge cutbacks were made in all the statewide educational systems that I could have contributed to. Back to Basics was in. Electives were out, and so was I.

Needless to say, this was a serious blow to my career, as I then perceived it. In truth, I really wasn't trained to do much of anything else.

Except play music. And there wasn't much money to be made in that field.

What to do?

One of my teachers, a poet named Charles Olson, used to say that "a man's (or woman's) work is to be creative. If you aren't being creative, you ought to be productive. If you aren't being productive, you should be making love. Anything else is a waste of time."

Playing music the way I played music qualified as making love, so I opted to take a short sabbatical before accepting a graduate fellowship at the School of Library Sciences. I had a month before the new semester began, and I wanted to play some music on the West Coast before getting back to my studies.

I left on a cold and snowy morning from New York, with a trumpet, guitar and backpack. I got off the plane in San Francisco, felt the 70º warmth, saw the blue sky and thought I had died and gone to heaven.

The date was November 11, 1969. Armistice Day. I declared a truce with New York and said hello to my new home.

I didn't know how, but I knew then that I'd never go back!

I knew only two names of people from Buffalo that I could even call on. One of them was in residence at the University of California at Santa Cruz, which, not coincidentally, had a library containing one of the most complete collections in the world of engravings by my mentor, William Blake. I promised myself that I would visit this shrine before returning east.

Hitchhiking was still reasonably safe in those days, and oftentimes downright stimulating. I'll never forget the time... oh, that's another whole story.

In any case, my last ride told me that where I really wanted to go was to a place called Bridge Mountain Foundation, a sort of small-scale Esalen, and a flagship of the human potential movement.

I took them up on their suggestion. And acting upon that impulse changed my life for good — and definitely for the better.

Precisely as I was walking up their driveway I was met by one of their staff who asked me, "Are you the person looking for the job?"

"No," I replied, "but if you're offering, I'll take it!"

Visions and Decisions

It happened so fast that I wasn't really sure it had really transpired. But then he said, "Come back in two hours and meet the rest of the staff. You can hang out in the redwood grove down the road in the meantime."

I followed his directions, and soon found myself in a forest that qualified as "enchanted" by all criteria I knew.

I remember being overcome with a strong

desire to sit down and meditate. It was like a wind blowing through me, and different than a conscious decision. Suddenly I found myself in some other time and space... and I was hearing music I had never heard before.

In that instant, I received the vision of what my life's work was to be.

The only problem was, there was no field of New Age meditative healing music— and much less a market for it.

The lesson for me was clear: There are times in our lives that we can indeed control and create our opportunities, and there are other times that are "bigger than both of us." We are being breathed by life, danced by life, and our job is to remain open to whatever is for the highest good.

There is a great deal of trust involved in "letting go and letting God" — but as we all begin to tap into the plan for our lives, who is to know that our calling to be a Mover, Shaker and Change Agent wasn't that which we chose before we decided to play this game of life this time around.

That day, I learned a great lesson about myself: I could surrender to a higher authority, or at least cooperate with it, and we'd all come out winners.

Noise Pollution is a Social Disease

I was quite young when I began to recognize that I responded to many of the noises in my environment in ways that others didn't. Or at least didn't appear to. I noticed that my Irritation Quotient (I.Q.) was much higher than many people's.

For example, when my family was eating dinner in our kitchen, I was always the one who complained that the noise from the refrigerator was disturbing my digestion.

But back then, in the immortal words of Rodney Dangerfield, I "got no respect." My father told me, "Ignore it, and it will go away. Besides, it's invisible, odorless and I don't hear it. Therefore it can't be affecting you!"

Such logic was unquestioned in those days by most parents that I knew. I began to question my own sanity, however, and started researching the field of psychoacoustics at an early age.

The results of that investigation of the medical literature proved conclusively that not only was I perfectly sane, but that many other people respond in similar ways. My research demonstrated that all bodies repond in similar ways to sound, although not all people are as sensitive to noticing it. More-over, many people are reluctant to admit that they are being made uncomfortable, fearing that they'd be ridiculed

In the years since I was thrust into this field, I have established my presence as one of the leading authorities on how sound and noise affect human beings. In so doing, I have helped countless thousands of people feel better about themselves, as they have been empowered to come out of the closet to live more fully enjoyable lives.

How To Be The Role Model

I have done this be writing numerous articles and several books, including TUNING THE HUMAN INSTRUMENT and SOUND HEALTH (Harper & Row). But I have also done this by example. Armed with the ammunition provided by my studies, I felt even more justified in standing up for my own rights — and, not coincidentally, for the rights of others.

For instance: As a professional speaker, I do a great deal of travelling, and have the opportunity to eat in many restaurants. I never cease to be amazed at how noisy many of these are, or how loud— and fast— the music is.

A little observation will attest to the veracity of this statement: You are wasting your money— and rendering your digestive system virtually inoperative — when you eat in a noisy environment. Loud, fast music, with or without noise, inhibits the flow of gastric juices. Not only that, you chew at the same speed as the background music. That's why I call this the "Eat to the Beat" phenomenon. Such environments also make it difficult to think creative thoughts, or to carry on a business discussion, let alone an intimate personal conversation.

For all these reasons, I have often found myself taking matters into my own hands. Now, mind you, I don't go looking for a fight. If the restaurant sounds like a football stadium, I turn around immediately. But all too often, the music and noise change radically after I've ordered, often in the middle of the entree.

When Noise Is On The Menu

I walk from table to table, enquiring of the other diners whether the music is offensive to them. Most readily concur. I invite them to sign my petition. (A napkin will work.) Remember, in unity there is strength. My most effective and dramatic successes occurred when I presented the maitre d' with a tablecloth signed by twenty patrons! I have always succeeded in getting the music changed to something more appropriate, and often contribue one of my own tapes to the cause, much to the delight and applause of my fellow patrons.

I don't know why no one else has thought of it, but I did, and in so doing, made a difference. You can do it too, when noise is on the menu. It's as easy as pie. And for dessert, you won't need antacids.

Changing The Face Of Modern Music

But by far the most significant "moving and shaking" I have done in my career has evolved out of my own need to give form to the creative forces inside me. I can only begin to touch the surface of expressing the pleasure and fulfillment that my work has afforded me. Thousands of letters over the years have let me know that I have also touched the lives of countless others. It is a gift I am honored and humbled to acknowledge.

I wasn't setting out to revolutionize the world of modern composition when I began. I found myself inexplicably drawn to the piano — an instrument I had never formally studied — and was fascinated by the music that tran- spired. So were my friends, who asked for tapes which I produced one at a time.

Clearly, this was not cost-or time-effective, especially since most recipients accepted the tape as a "gift." Their feedback, however, proved that there was a need and a market for music that could help the listener achieve a calm and centered state that felt wonderful, was legal, non-addictive, inexpensive, and could be used at home!

The healing and therapeutic value of music has been known for millennia. It is, after all, the most ancient of the "healing arts." But there was precious little literature or research available that focused on the "relaxation response," and nowhere to purchase resources and software.
You wouldn't find it on the Top 40 and therefore, you wouldn't find it, even if it did exist, in record stores.

It was about that time that I realized that my heretofore "impractical" liberal arts background was all coming together to provide me with the perfect base of operations. The psychology, sociology, biology, philosophy and physics all made sense now, in light of the larger picture of understanding how sound and music affect us as psycho-physiological beings. I could draw on my training to validate and give credibility to the field, and to the music.

My job description suddenly expanded exponentially. Getting the music was the easy part. Communicating it to others was the challenge. I would have to establish the existence of a new field - a new age of music - and then create a pipeline of distribution for products that had never existed before in venues that had never sold such products before.

This was all a bit overwhelming to me at first. As a child of the sixties, anything smacking of business was suspect. And musicians were notorious for being non-business minded. My options were to learn business; ie, to learn the marketplace as an instrument, or starve. Given that range of options, my path was clear.

However, there wasn't anyone else doing what I was doing, so there wasn't anyone I could seek out as a role model. I put bits and pieces together from a variety of sources and set myself up as Halpern Sounds, an independent record company. Our focus was specific: To create and produce music that was beautiful, relaxing, and a positive conribution to the lives of others, no matter what their lifestyle.

Educating My Audience

I quickly discovered that it was often necessary to

educate others to get some moving and shaking done. For instance, I assumed that health food stores, because they served people who were concerned about their health, would be an obvious place to position my recordings. I assumed the owners would agree. Instead, they balked. They said that they only sold vegetables, or vitamins, and that my records and tapes were neither.

I countered by explaining that music was really "vitamins of the airwaves." Just as light had been proven to be a nutrient, so too had sound. We all need a minimum daily dose of healthy sound. If we lived in a noisy environment, we needed to supplement our diet. That's where the music came in. I suggested to them that they were not just in the "health food business," but in the lifestyle support business. People who shopped in their stores did so to find all sorts of products that would support their healthy lifestyles.

Now, ten years later, health food stores have become one of the mainstays of the alternative music scene. Titles by a multitude of artists abound. The downside was that I no longer had the field to myself, but the upside was that a transformation took place, and the benefits are there for all to enjoy.

A similar situation transpired with bookstores. Now, not only specialty stores, but major chain stores carry music cassettes and do a brisk business. It was not an overnight transformation, and it took the work of many individuals to get to the present point, but I was the first to break the ice, and I take pride in my role as a "change agent." The field of New Age music received its first Grammy award for the 1986 season, further testimony to the growing presence of the "healthy" trend in contemporary adult music.

Moving and Shaking to Your Own Rhythm

Many of us are familiar with the saying, "Physician, heal thyself." This might be paraphrased: "Movers and shakers, move and shake yourself." It's certainly true that you can't move someone else if you can't get yourself moving.

How do you get yourself moving? Or if you're already in motion, how might you optimize your efficiency? I'd like to offer several sound suggestions. You're sure to find some that will strike a responsive chord within you. At that point, they are yours for the rest of your life. Stay tuned!

As I spell out in my book, *SOUND HEALTH*, researchers have documented that certain kinds of sounds, whether they are music or noise, contribute to stress, tension, lack of concentration and decreased productivity. What is even more fascinating is that they can do this even if we "like" them, or are not even aware of them.

Nature gave us eyelids, but she didn't give us earlids. Our bodies and minds continually respond to the sounds around us. Thus, it makes sense to bring your personal and professional audio environs into a format that supports who you are, and what you need to keep in top shape.

1. A simple way to begin is to quiet the volume of your own sounds. Loud sounds trigger a stress response. Ask your neighbors to do the same with their tv's, stereos, etc.

2. Get out in nature. Listen to the symphony of life around you. The birds, ocean or lake that you hear have balanced and healed people for millennia. They are part of the Celestial Top 40 that never go out of date.

3. Bring more beautiful music into your life. There is so much good music to choose from, one hardly knows there to start. Assemble a library of music that gets your juices moving. You can ask your friends for suggestions, but be forewarned: The same music may not work for you. There's no right or wrong, just what works. You should include choices for several purposes, such as "music for inspiration," "music for enhancing productivity and creativity," "music to get you motivated," and "music for relaxing and recharging."

If your lifestyle doesn't include at least 20 minutes a day specifically set aside for relaxation, you are missing out on a vital ingredient in your optimal performance, high-level wellness program. The research from the medical community is very clear on this. The right kinds of music in your life can literally assist your body in healing itself, and give you the foundation from which to do anything more effectively.

Relaxation makes available to the body untapped resources of energy and creativity. A simple way to tap into the relaxation response is to use music specifically composed for that purpose.

Three selections that work for me are *DAWN, NATURAL LIGHT, AND SPECTRUM SUITE.*

Motivating the Motivator

For fifteen years, I have been dealing with the question of what to do if you REALLY want to fine-tune tapes to get them to work for YOU. I've discovered that by taking two of the primary modalities of accessing consciousness, namely self-talk/positive affirmation, and music, we can achieve wonders.

Many people have discovered the power of positive thinking. Others have discovered the power of positive speaking, to oneself, through the vehicle of affirmation. Most people have not, however, gone the next step— putting their own personal affirmation onto tape. Of those who have, fewer still have combined them with appropriate music to fully maximize the effect.

Recent research suggests that there is an even more potent way to access the power of the mind— by speaking to the subconscious mind through subliminal programming. There is nothing mysterious about this: Olympic athletes and top executives have been using it for years. Indeed, we do it all the time to ourselves, without even knowing it.

Any time you say to yourself, "I can't do that," "This will never work," or "I can't lose weight," you are programming your subconscious mind to fail.

Why not program it to succeed?

There are many tapes on the market that have ready-made messages with a wide variety of topics. The quality varies, but the principle is amazingly effective.

Recording Your Own

What if you want to say something that isn't available, or tailor the affirmations to your personal needs? Have no fear; Halpern's Rx for personalizing the tapes is here.

Step one: The ingredients are simple. You'll need two tape decks, one of which can record. Depending on your budget, you can upgrade, or get together with audiophile friends. But the benefits from any level of production will be evident, so jump on in.

Step two is to write your script, your list of positive affirmations. Typically these will be short sentences or phrases, such as "I am a mover and a shaker;" "I am a success." You might also include your name; "I, _____, am a successful speaker." Alternatives could be in the second person, "You are totally relaxed." Write as many as you like, or just repeat a single statement.

Step three involves choosing the music you want to accompany your affirmation. I recommend trying two varieties: One of the up-tempo genre, and one of the anti-frantic style. The principle here is that the music shouldn't be so intellectually or emotionally interesting as to distract you from the affirmation.

Once you have assembled the raw materials, go into the quietest room of your home. (Hint: To enhance the resonance of your voice, do the recording in the bathroom. The hard tile surfaces typically make you sound better than any other room. Plus, you can add sound effects such as the shower if you desire.)

The key is to experiment with your closeness to the microphone relative to the speaker playing back the music so that the blend of voice and music works for you. Getting there is half the fun.

Once you have your position set, take a deep breath, and do at least ten minutes of non-stop recording.

Then give yourself a week of playing the tape at least once a day before you make any adjustments or do your next recording.

The Next Step

You can take this one step further by making subliminal tapes. According to many authorities the easiest way to access deeper levels of the subconscious mind is to bypass the conscious mind, which may offer resistance to certain concepts you wish to encode.

To make your own subliminal tapes, repeat all of the above steps, with this modification: You will need to adjust the blend of voice and music to be virtually 99% music. Move further from the microphone, or speak more softly. The goal is to barely, if at all, hear your voice. But rest assured, the message will get through.

Pay attention to your coefficient of success with these sound-assisted techniques for moving and shaking yourself into the peak performer you are. I'd be most interested in hearing of your experiences. Please feel free to write me with feedback, comments, questions or requests for free brochures of recommended music.

In the meanwhile, stay tuned to the Mover and Shaker within you.

See deep enough, and you see musically; the heart of nature being everywhere music, if you can only reach it. - Carlyle

PATRICIA BALL
Patricia Ball Corporate Communications
9875 Northbridge Road
St. Louis, MO 63124
(3l4)966-5452 (3l4)966-5457

Patricia Ball

Patricia Ball, CSP, nationally acclaimed professional speaker, communications specialist, and entertainer, has been involved in providing programs and seminars across the country for over 15 years. Her offerings cover two distinctly different areas: Keynotes, programs and seminars on various aspects of communication for corporations, associations and general business meetings; and costumed theatrical performances in which she portrays a variety of women, both real and fictional.

Because of Patricia's background as a professional actor - television, radio and on the stage - she brings to her communications programs a unique flair for visual illustration. Her ability to demonstrate specific techniques and scenarios is a recognized trademark for her talent in delivering ideas to her audience. This highly interactive format strongly supports the proven theory that a "picture is worth a thousand words."

A long-time member of the National Speakers Association, Patricia was also a charter president and co-founder of the St. Louis-Gateway Chapter of NSA, is a member of Actors Equity Association and The American Federation of Television and Radio Artists and a board member of Sales & Marketing Executives of St. Louis. The National Speakers Association has awarded her the coveted Certified Speaking Professional (CSP) designation of achievement. Patricia is listed in the World Who's Who of Women and 2000 Notable Americans.

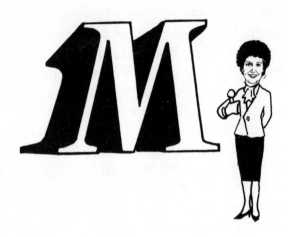

All the World's a Stage -
People and the Roles They Play

By Patricia Ball

All the world's a stage
And all the men and women merely players:
They have their exits and their entrances:
And one man in his time plays many parts.
                        -William Shakespeare

William Shakespeare, one of the greatest movers, shakers and change makers of all time, was certainly a very perceptive person. As he so brilliantly observed, all the world is a stage. I am a professional actor, speaker and communications specialist. I deal with people each and every day of my life. So do you. We're both called upon to play roles to many audiences. How we play these roles — with what degree of honesty and understanding — is the measure of our effectiveness and, in the long run, of our success.

An actor's success depends upon how well he or she communicates a role to the audience. So does yours, especially if you are in the people business. Success involves how well you understand the people with whom you come in daily contact and how well they understand you.

An actor's concerns in communicating the playwright's meaning are very much the same as your concerns in dealing with your worlds of people. Communicating is so much more than the words themselves! It's *how* we say them, *when* we say them, how we *mean* them. It's how they're interpreted. It's the expressions on our faces; it's even our silences.

To perform my trade effectively, I must learn (1) to understand *self*, (2) to understand *others*, and, finally (3) to use the mechanical devices that help to get this understanding across to the audience — body language, voice, and intonations. I am going to share with you some of the tools I use to arrive at the essence of the characters I depict. It might surprise you to discover that these same tools are extremely useful in your own daily people encounters.,

I will speak in terms of the actor who has a role to portray to an audience. However, throughout, comparisons may be drawn to situations common in your own life, whether an attempt to close a sale, dealing with an employee problem, or any basic face-to-face confrontation.

Know the Audience

To begin, an actor is usually selected for a role because of physical characteristics that fit a playwrights's character description. He or she must show at least some surface understanding of the role and have the training required for interpreting the role successfully. (Similarly, *you* have been selected for your role in sales, management, etc., because you meet certain standard requirements.)

After the selection process is complete and the play is cast, the director schedules rehearsals. Preliminary rehearsals are geared to an overall understanding of the play and the playwright's intent, and to knowledge of the audience and how the playwright wants to "touch" that audience. These issues will be valuable ones for you to consider, also: Who is the audience? What is their identity? How can I project these meanings and emotions to the audience? How can I share with them?

As an actor I learned early to recognize the differences between audiences and to adapt my techniques accordingly. During the six-day presentation of a given play, I may have to alter my

performance radically to fit the changing tempera-
ments of the audience. If I am good at my craft, I
will be able to adapt my interpretation to a particular audience without once being false to the basic
design.

So the first step an actor must take is to know
the audience, just as you must know your audience. The second step is to understand the play,
as you must understand your product or job. You
might think of the script for a play as being like a
score for a musical. Like music, a play must be
translated into sensible forms — living bodies,
voices, motion, scenery, costumes, lighting, and
sound effects. In the initial rehearsal period I try
to understand the audience, the play, and the
character I am to enact, as well as to fully
understand *myself* in that context.

Understanding Ourselves

It is necessary that we understand ourselves before we can understand others. Why is this so? I
might at some point in my career find myself
unable to play a character convincingly because
that character touches upon an area of blindness
within me. Similarly, you, in your own setting,
could find yourself unable to communicate with
another person because of some blind spot of your
own that functions as a block to understanding.

Since we first must be honest with ourselves,
it takes real courage to understand others. A noted

psychologist once said that he can be helpful to another person only if he can *permit* himself to understand that person. He then pointed out the significance of the word *permit* — that if one undertakes to genuinely understand another, he or she runs a risk of being changed in the process! What this psychologist is talking about is the "selves" of ourselves, as described by the Johari Window.

(*See following page*)

The Johari Window was developed by Joseph Luft and Harry Ingham. In the accompanying illustration I adapt the information found in it to theatrical terms. You can apply the same principles to your audience. Notice that as the ovals widen the actor gets deeper and deeper into character development. He or she also digs deeper and deeper into self understanding and, as a result, is able to touch, involve, or *sell* the audience.

Let's briefly define these selves:

1. First, there is the *open self* or the common area, a part of us known both to us and the common area of an interrelationship.

2. Our *concealed self* is that part of us which we tend to hide from others — our very private world, as in our insecurities. These are the attitudes, feelings, and values that we don't reveal.

3. Our *blind self* is that part unknown to us of which others are aware. This has to do with those things we could see and even understand if we would *just let ourselves* — our fears and prejudices, for example.

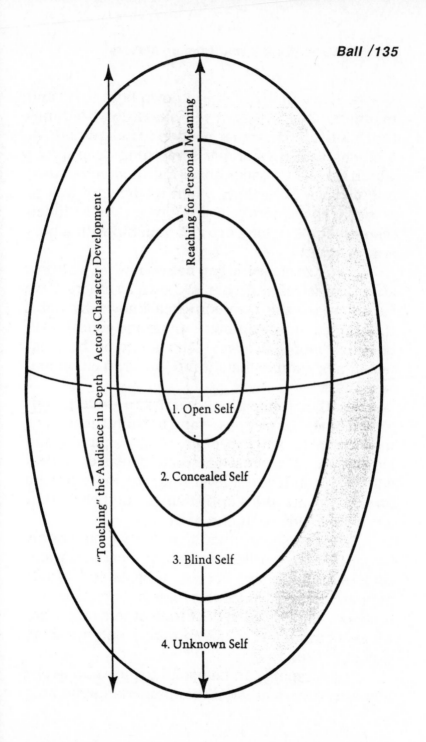

1. Open Self

2. Concealed Self

3. Blind Self

4. Unknown Self

4. The fourth self is unknown both to us and to others. Our *unknown self* has to do with things that motivate us which we don't understand. It includes that mysterious something deep inside which starts our knees knocking, stomach churning, or voice squeaking when we have to talk to someone in authority. (Does it represent a hidden memoryline to a long ago relationship with a parent, or what?)

If we can close the gap between what we know about ourselves and what is known by others, if we can increase the common area known by both, then our communications — mine and yours — will be much more effective. This is one of the great benefits of gaining insight into our own emotional responses.

Another tremendous barrier to understanding others is stereotypes — and not only those we're most familiar with through public opinion and legislation. These may actually be easier to deal with on an individual level than the more private ones — the attitudes and feelings and beliefs that are deep inside each one of us.

These misconceptions, which we commonly acquire at the earliest stages of awareness and understanding, have become a basic part of our personalities. They inhibit honest, open communication, causing us to hear from others only what we expect to hear, to see in others only what we expect to see.

Stereotyping can be useful to me as an actor. Adapting a few stereotypical mannerisms can help in the portrayal of certain types of characters. But it's also true that my own built-in biases and prejudices can prevent me from interpreting a character effectively.

Whether we are trying to persuade one person or a thousand, we must force ourselves to see through the stereotypes we've built in our minds. We must overcome our blind spots so that we can project our feelings and selves onto others. And that is the next challenge.

Identification

After we have become somewhat aware of ourselves, with our insecurities and blind spots, the next step is to attempt to move and be moved by others, to portray a situation with validity and to convince the audience to accept it as a reality. To do this we must first have some common element, some means of identifying with the people we wish to convince. Success depends largely upon the associated meanings, feelings, and emotions we stir in them.

In one of the many programs I present nation-wide, I play the part of a fifteen-year-old black girl who attempted to go to Central High School in Little Rock, Arkansas, in 1954, when there was great resistance to the Supreme Court Desegregation ruling. Seated at center stage, I perform an actual account of this young girl's day. I am not black, it's been some time since I was fifteen, and I have never been the object of racial discrimination. How, then can I bring my audience to understand, to feel, to become involved?

As any communicator must do, I must make myself aware of some common bond in our experiential or emotional backgrounds. I must search through my experience so that I can fully understand the character. I must ask: *How am I like this person?*

From my memory I dredged up a past hurt. Many years ago, when I was a new girl in high school and a good dancer, I was asked to entertain at a school dance. I arrived in blue jeans, a shirt, and loafers and went immediately into the ladies room to change into my costume. From the stall I overheard two students talking about "the poor little new girl" who didn't know any better than to come to a dance in jeans.

I was deeply hurt and felt very misunderstood. I was mortified! With a sinking, sick feeling in the pit of my stomach, I summoned up all the courage that I could muster to step out of the stall. (The girls stopped talking instantly, looked flustered, and left in a big hurry!)

This is the experience I chose to make use of in depicting the role of the young black girl. I relived and tried to magnify the discrimination I had felt many years ago as a newcomer at school. I tried to imagine the terror that she had experienced. I tried to summon up the bravery that it took on her part to face that crowd of haters. Thus I was able to recreate for my audience her inner tumult. I was able to *empathize* and put myself in her place.

Empathy is a sensuous response which involves the whole self, physical as well as mental. It's similar to the participation experienced by a spectator at a sports event. It's breaking through to the feeling level. You can see that in order to do this you have to have a certain amount of awareness and understanding of others.

Nonverbal Communication

Now that we have taken some first steps toward understanding ourselves and understanding others, how do we communicate that understanding to our audience? The actor's mediums of communication are three:

1. Words, excluding their tone coloring
2. External body movement, posturing and gesturing
3. Voice-tones

To get your audience to respond takes far more than the words themselves. It has been said that item two, which includes the nonverbal area of body language — facial expressions, the way you sit or stand, whether you're looking at a person or not, posture, the way you dress, constitutes 70 percent of all communications. In fact, if we were to consider voice tones, including pitch, quality, and rate, as part of this category, then perhaps as much as 97 percent of all communication is nonverbal.

Body language is, for the most part, unconscious. It is the most honest form of communication. We can easily lie with words, but an astute observer will be able to discover the lie by reading our body signals. What the voice doesn't say, the body does. Sometimes it says it all!

Blocking

Nonverbal communication is especially important to an actor, as the playwright is responsible for choosing the words. Body language is at the very core of acting.

This brings us to the second step in putting together a piece of drama. We have progressed through the first few rehearsals of the play. We have attempted to discover our own blind spots in relation to our roles. We have tried to delve into the workings of the character and attempted to understand what makes the character (and ourselves) tick. In this next rehearsal stage we must somehow get this understanding across to our audience.

"Blocking" is how the characters move on stage in relation to one another. These are not ironclad rules. While a body movement means one thing in a particular setting, it doesn't necessarily follow that it will mean the same thing in all settings. Generally, however, many of the following meanings apply.

On stage, as in real life, a piece of furniture separating two persons is not only a physical barrier, but also an *emotional* barrier. It will keep two communicators apart. You might consider this when you attempt to have a meaningful dialogue with a work-mate. Select a chair by the side of the desk, if there's one available, rather than directly in front.

Sitting at a 45-degree angle, with knees facing the other person, is the position most conducive to compatible conversation. On the other hand, if two characters in a play are at odds with each other, they might place themselves squarely in front of and facing each other, a position of confrontation. If, in your people dealings, you want to avoid the impression of disagreement or confrontation, you would be wise to choose a stance other than squarely facing the other person with weight evenly distributed on both feet.

In a scene where you need to *listen* intently to what is being said, assume a listening stance, a mirror image of the person with whom you are in conversation. If the other person leans forward in her chair, you lean forward, too. (Leaning forward denotes intensity and interest.) You two are then in harmony, and you convey the message, "I am as one with you — I am listening!"

It would impart quite a different body language message to lean back in your chair. This could be interpreted as disinterest, or even hostility, toward what is being said.

Body Space

Body space is another important concept which I will touch on here only briefly. We all have space which forms an invisible circle around our bodies. This constitutes our area of privacy. We feel uncomfortable when someone invades this circle— unless, in our minds, we have given them permission to do so— as with a lover or close friend. Body space requirements differ from person to person and culture to culture.

Here are two different examples of body space used in an office setting. If I am portraying a timid secretary, I will knock gingerly on the door to the boss's office, perhaps step barely inside the door and talk to that person from across the room. At the other extreme, if I'm playing an aggressive boor, I might push open the boss's door without bothering to knock, walk right up to the desk, and lean threateningly into that character's body space.

In your day-to-day dealings, if a person takes a subtle step backwards as you approach, you might be encroaching upon that individual's body space. It might make sense to retreat.

Let's look at size for a minute. The height of an actor has significance not only in the types of parts one is given, but in how each part is played on stage. I am a tall woman. Because people frequently equate size with power, I have been fortunate over the years to have been selected for some very important roles— on stage and off. But height can also be a detriment. Picture a real-life scene in which a very tall person applies for a job and the employer or personnel director is very short. In this situation you should sit down as soon as possible!

Rising and Falling

The whole area of body movement narrows down to two basic considerations: rising, approaching actions and sinking, withdrawing actions. Rising energy is reflected in a lift of the body, ebbing energy in a drooping body. Upward movement is associated with life — a growing plant, a young child, a person of vigor. Downward movement is related to death—the sick, the weary, and the discouraged. The fundamental rising-sinking action is executed on stage either as a lift or fall of the entire body or of single body members.

For the most part, the motivation behind body movements comes from within, from our inner feelings and emotions. But it is possible to consciously change an inner feeling by changing the outward body language manifestation. How you walk communicates an image to a viewer. A talented young actor can walk on stage and project a person of eighty without saying a single word. Conversely, a skilled older actor can project youth with body movements — in the first instance sinking, and in the second rising.

On a day when you are depressed, try to put a spring into your gait. Quicken your step and lift your stomach, chest, and rib cage. Hold your head erect, and smile. This positive physical action actually might cause you to feel less dejected. (Use this simple technique for your next job interview, after a number of unsuccessful ones, or for your next sales pitch after a week of no sales.)

Muscular Tension

Another important tool of the actor is muscular tension and relaxation. Try tensing many of the muscles in your body all at once and see what happens to your mood. If you do this over a period of time, you will feel uptight and edgy and present this image to others. On the other hand, thinking *relaxation* into your muscles helps in the outward appearance of serenity and assurance.

How you sit tells a great deal about your feelings. How far forward do you like to sit? Not only does leaning forward show intensity and interest in the other person, it also displays self-confidence. These things will come to you unconsciously if you believe in yourself. Otherwise, that disbelief will show up in body language to betray you.

Gestures

Gestures play a very important part in the development of a character. All too often, gestures present a negative meaning. Tugging at an earlobe, chewing a lip, and playing with a strand of hair all transmit the message, "I am ill at ease"— which is fine if you're playing the part of a submissive clerk being bawled out by the boss. However, it's not so good if you happen to be presenting next year's sales forecast at a large meeting. These gestures draw people's attention and prevent them from listening.

Using the Voice

We are now well along into the production process of a play. We have laboriously delved into our inner selves in relationship with others, and we have studied others in order to be able to empathize. We have blocked our movements on stage, and we have worked on our body language and gestures. The next step is to develop our vocal tones, not only as befits our character, but in order to clearly convey to the audience the meaning of the words. Again, I am asking you to think of yourself as an actor, because this information applies to those situations in which you will want *your* voice to work well.

It is very easy for an actor to learn the words of a script, but without tone these words have little meaning; they are barren of expression. Tone is the *color* of speech. It is the inflection of your voice. There's an angry *no*, a *no* which implies command, a mischievous *no*, an inviting *no*, and a *no* which really means yes. Examine the next five sentences and imagine a tone of voice that will convey a meaning exactly *opposite* to the words themselves.

- What an "interesting" dessert.
- I just *love* to take out the garbage!
- Of course I love you!
- Dammit, I'm not angry!
- You just trumped my ace, *sweetheart!*

Tone is the emotion indicator in your voice. Without tone your voice will be monotonous and unemotional. You'll want to train your voice in such a way that it will be flexible, colorful, strong, varied, and impressive. Words must also be spoken clearly and articulately. The four basic factors in vocal tone are *pitch, speed, volume,* and *timbre.*

Pitch represents tonal level. Generally speaking, the lower pitch levels are richer and deeper in color and more pleasing to the ear. Higher tonal levels are sometime necessary, as in the expression of excitement or great cheerfulness. However, they usually give a thinner sound, so it is important to make sure the voice is well modulated in those higher tones (unless, of course, you are playing a part that requires thinness of voice— perhaps a weak or frightened character). The wider your range of pitch levels, the more interesting your voice will be. For the most part, tonal variety will cause you to be a person to whom others will listen.

The second factor in vocal tone has to do with tempo. In the words of Hamlet, "Speak the speech, I pray you, as I pronounced it to you — trippingly on the tongue." The normal speech rate is from 140 to l60 words a minute. For everyday speech either an overly fast or an overly slow rate will create a negative response in your listener.

Volume of speech, of course, has to do with loudness, softness, and intensity— or vocal pressure. Be aware of the reactions of others when you speak. If other people are constantly asking "What was that?" "Could you repeat that?" or, "I'm sorry, I didn't hear you," then you need to add more volume to your voice. On the other hand, if people often seem to flinch when you speak, then you might try to use softer voice tones.

Timbre of voice has to do with the changing qualities (softness, hardness, smoothness, and brittleness). For instance, gruff or harsh vocal sounds may communicate more hostility or aggression than is intended, just as silky, smooth tones might disguise those same qualities.

Breath Control

One of the actor's continuing battles is in mastering breath control. This is important to you, as well, because at some time in your life, if not frequently as a part of your job, you may be called upon to speak to a large group. Without proper breath control you will not be heard. Your voice will sound tired and old, and you will be plagued by hoarseness, sore throat, and laryngitis. Most faults of the speaking voice are due to incorrect breathing. Control won't make you sound like Judith Anderson or Orson Welles, but it will help you sound like the best possible you!

The first step in proper breathing is to learn to relax. Before going "on stage" in your arena of the conference or meeting room, take a deep breath. Then exhale as slowly and steadily as possible. Do this several times. Also open your mouth and yawn a few times.

The next consideration is good posture. Keep your chest up, your stomach in. If you're standing, keep your weight evenly distributed on the balls of your feet. When you stand with rounded shoulders, so that your chest is caved in, it doesn't take a great deal of insight to know what happens to the diaphragm and chest cavity. It's difficult to draw a proper supply of air into those cramped quarters. The lungs cannot fully expand. (When I want to depict a character who is tired, depressed, and beaten, one of the first techniques I use is to collapse my diaphragm area. Not only will this affect my physical appearance, but it actually makes my voice appear listless and weak. So remember, stomach in, chest out!)

Controlling the breath is really a matter of controlling the contractions of the muscles around the diaphragm so that breath is forced out of the chest cavity in a *smooth, steady* stream. We have been told many times to breathe from the diaphragm, but this is really inaccurate. It's actually the intercostal muscles surrounding the diaphragm that do much of the work. Dorothy Sarnoff, in her book *Speech Can Change Your Life*, calls these muscles "the girdle of breath support." These muscles exert pressure on the diaphragm and cause an air current to pass from your lungs up your windpipe and through all your speech apparatus (vocal cords, nasal passages, and mouth). It comes out as sound.

To locate the "girdle of breath support" and the diaphragm, place the palm of your hand flat on the area about three inches above your navel, at the bottom of your rib cage. Now take a deep breath and exhale slowly. See what happens to that area.

Again, Dorothy Sarnoff helps us understand the principles of breath support with a quote from the famous opera singer, Giovanni Martinelli. "Think," he would say, " of a Ping-pong ball bobbing on the crest of a fountain. Imagine that the ball is your voice and that the fountain is the breath supporting it. If the support remains undiminished, the ball will bob there indefinitely, but if the support slackens, the ball will drop away."

Here are two exercises for developing good breath control. Work on them for five to ten minutes a day.

1. Take a deep breath and see how far you can count. Eventually you should be able to count to 60 on the exhalation of one breath.

2. Take a deep breath and exhale slowly, issuing a constant flow of the sound *sss* while someone counts aloud. Remember that proper breath control is not as much a matter of how much air you take in, as of how you support it on the way out.

I have done a great deal of recording work. When I first started out, one of my greatest problems was that the microphone in a recording studio, being a very sensitive device would pick up my breathing sounds. I was taking in huge gulps of air in what should come across as silent pauses. It took me a while to learn to do it properly. A sip of air is all you need to speak a long phrase or sentence. Learn to take quick "catch" breaths through the mouth.

Strong support is essential for voice projection, or carrying power. Most of the time when you are called upon to speak in your business life, a microphone will be supplied. You might think that projection is not necessary with a microphone. Not so! Microphones are fallible. They do go awry, and the occasion may arise when you have to use your "naked" voice. It's best to be prepared by having a trained voice and good breath control to back it up.

Costumes

Now it's dress rehearsal night and we are beginning to costume for our parts. If what we wear were not a significant part of the communications process, actors would not be required to wear costumes. Costumes are very important in conveying the character an actor plays. Similarly, the clothes *you* wear define you in many different ways — nonconformist, conformist, self-confident, or insecure.

For example, consider ex-President Carter's casual dress during his first fireside chat, as contrasted with his later formal attire when the country obviously needed a sense of confidence in leadership. How will the corporate president be viewed by his directors if he attends the board meeting dressed in the same sweater and blue jeans that he wore to the plant employees' meeting Saturday morning? How does IBM perceive its customers, when it requires more formal dress from its sales representative.?

It is obvious from these examples that intent should be reinforced by appearance when you don't wish to risk giving false signals. On the other hand, if the objective is not to reveal your intentions too soon, then dress can serve as a convenient mask. (When you are on the receiving end, you must be sure to look behind the clothing facade to perceive accurate meanings).

Opening Night

Are you ready for encore after encore? If you have tried to understand the inner you, learned to know your audience and empathize with them, become technically more proficient in the skills of the communicator, and dressed for the part, you can be sure that the results will show!

Instead of being "a poor player that struts and frets his hour upon the stage and then is heard no more" (Shakespeare's *Macbeth*), you will be a "well grace'd actor, leaving the stage" (Shakespeare's *Richard II*).

RON USELDINGER, M.A
National Director
Fitness Motivation Institute of America
36 Harold Avenue
San Jose, CA 95117
(408) 246-9191

Ronald E. Useldinger, M.A.

Ron Useldinger is one of the nation's most sought-after convention speakers. He has traveled over one million miles evangelizing the positive benefits of being physically fit. His new book "ISOROBICS - A Better Way to Fitness" has been a big success. He has also written articles for national magazines and has appeared on many leading TV talk shows throughout the country. Ron has a Masters Degree in Physical Education, and is, himself, an award winning high school and college athlete. A dynamic motivator as a coach, his high school teams in football and wrestling won several major championships in California.

Ron is a member of the Association for Fitness in Business and Industry, National Strength Coaches Association, and has served on the AAU Council on Physical Fitness. In addition, he is a CSP (Certified Speaking Professional) member of the National Speakers Association and is listed in Who's Who in Business and Industry of America. He also serves as the President of his own company, Fitness Motivation Institute of America.

Ron has been a conditioning consultant for many of the top professional sports teams, including the 49ers, Raiders, Seahawks, Warriors, Mariners, and many others. He has produced several one half hour TV specials on Physical fitness which are shown frequently throughout the United States.

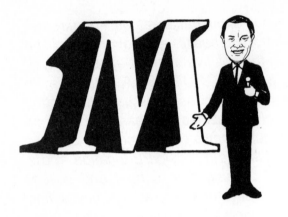

Change Your Life Through The Power of Physical Fitness

By Ron Useldinger, M.A.

Do you not know that your body is a temple of the Holy Spirit within you… So glorify God in your body."
I Cor. 6:19,20

My face to face encounter with my own mortality was not a dramatic event like a terrible automobile accident or diagnosis of a terminal illness. My brush with death at 30 years of age was an internal process which occured on New Year's Day. I looked at myself in the mirror and didn't like what I saw.

From a healthy football player of 185 pounds,

I had allowed my weight to slowly creep up to a flabby 215 pounds. I was out of shape and really out of control. My manly figure of broad shoulders and narrow waist had reversed itself.

While I stared at myself in the bathroom mirror, I knew that what I was doing to my body was going to hasten my death. I was tired at noon, and asleep in front of the television by eight in the evening. I didn't like what I saw, I was deeply unhappy.

I was out of the habit of physical exercise. I knew that to really take proper care of my body I had to get into a pattern as automatic as brushing my teeth and combing my hair.

Before I even began to consider what I might do to improve the terrible state into which my body had fallen, I knew all the drawbacks of exercise. I knew the boredom. I knew the fatigue and soreness. I knew how many people died on the first few days of the year as they suddenly attempted to reform their lives in an unrealistic resolve to make up, in a matter of days, what years of overeating and underexercising had caused.

Me, The High School Football Coach

That New Year's Day, I really took stock of the direction my life was headed. My priorities were God, family and work. Physical fitness wasn't even in the running! What made this so ironic was that I was employed as a high school football coach and really loved what I was doing. I had no trouble getting kids out on the field to work very hard two hours a day, week after week. Yet I did not take the time for myself. The hypocrisy of my body saying one thing while I mouthed another was suddenly too apparent to me. I was ashamed.

My mind reasoned over the problem. I had always thought I was a great motivator, but maybe I wasn't. For the first time, it occured to me that a person has to be self-motivated. Another person can attempt to inspire us, but there is no real action unless it comes from within. Those students didn't get out on the field day after day just because of my pep talks. They got out there because they enjoyed the game. If the season wasn't scheduled with challenges from rival football teams, I knew that within a couple of weeks there would be no one out on the field.

But I had no real motivation to change my ways. I was disgusted with the way I looked and felt. Even the prospect of losing my family and work prematurely, due to my excess fat and hardened arteries, didn't make me move.

Five Factors That Create Problems.

1.   **TIME.** One of the key problems for anyone like myself, who suddenly realizes he needs to change, is the problem of TIME. I'm not the only one who feels there are never enough hours in a day. Even my job as high school football coach was not providing the vigorous exercise that my body

needed. I knew it was foolhardy to attempt to fit into the weekends what I wasn't doing daily. Just as the first few days of January score an inordinate amount of fatal heart attacks for those who abruptly launch into something their bodies are ill-prepared for, the sharp rise of heart attacks on Saturdays and Sundays underlines a similar phenomena. It seemed impossible for me to allocate sufficient time on a daily basis. I wished for something that could be as automatic for me as shaving. But the habit was not there. Shaving took a lot less time than any exercise program I had ever heard of.

2. BOREDOM. Another prominent setback to my plans for an exercise program is the repetition which is intrinsically boring. We must keep increasing the number of any particular exercise to reap the same positive gains. For example, if I do five push-ups today, a year from now I must do 105 to reap the same benefits. Nothing good in terms of improvement or change takes place until the person exercising begins to tire. Cumulative buildup of exercises are necessary. But more and more repetition of the same exercise spells boredom.

3. SORENESS. Another major problem in exercise is SORENESS. Nobody had to tell me how stiff and sore one can get when a rigorous reform program is attempted. I have gotten out of bed after a few days of overdoing and exclaimed, "I'm in pain.

That's it. No more. I quit." What happened was a build up of lactic acid which is a simple by-product of working muscle.

Another type of soreness is the actual physical injuries that I could inflict on myself by an activity like jogging. I was already overweight. My extra weight would serve to add extra impact every time my foot hit the sidewalk. I would send a tremendous jolt to my ankles, knees, hips and lower back on every bounce. With every stride my weight was amplified from over 200 pounds to a staggering 600 pounds!

4. INCONVENIENCE. We live in a world where sitting fourteen hours a day is common. Getting the right exercise is downright INCONVENIENT. I knew all the reasons why it would be inconvenient for me. I didn't want to "suit up" and go out there and face the neighbors.

If I attemped to jog, I was sure I would be chased by every dog in the neighborhood. I thought nobody could see my problem. I wanted to keep my resolution to reform a secret. Wasn't there something I could do in the privacy of my own home? Maybe even in the closet?

I know for others there is also the problem of thinking of exercise in the form of a competitive sport. This idea really adds to the inconvenience! If you have to reserve a court and line up a partner for racquetball or tennis, it is much easier to procrastinate. Not everybody likes competitive sports, either.

So when I confronted myself on that January morning I had a new insight into MOTIVATION because of my own personal lack of it. I realized that instead of motivation coming from somebody else, *MOTIVATION MUST COME FROM WITHIN.* Every person has to find his or her own reason to exercise. My own reason was the recognition of what I would lose so soon if I did not get the regular healthful exercise my body desperately needed. I wanted to look good, feel good and be physically fit.

5. ENLIGHTENMENT. That month of January was difficult for me. I knew the problem but I didn't have a viable solution. I knew all the reasons why the conventional resolutions that most people make wouldn't work for me. I didn't have the "easy out" of fooling myself. I knew as a coach that easy solutions were unrealistic.

Fortunately, I was scheduled to attend a football clinic in Palo Alto at the end of January. Attending such a clinic is a rather standard activity for a football coach, so I did not enter that room with any expectation that what I would hear would be any more than coaching advice.

Three hours later I came out a changed man. I had a solution to my problem from a most unexpected source. You could even say the answer came to me from outer space!

At that particular clinic, scientists who worked for N.A.S.A. came and shared with us a small simple piece of equipment which the astronauts were using to exercise in our country's space program. As I watched the device being demonstrated, I was awestruck by the simple wisdom of the concept.

The Isorobic Exercise System

The piece of equipment these scientists had designed for the astronaut's use weighed less than two pounds, yet it rivaled the versatility of a gymnasium full of exercise equipment. When I had contemplated the idea of being a "closet exerciser" I had never considered the confined space in which astronauts must exercise to keep their bodies in optimum condition!

By adjusting a small dial, the demonstrators of the ISOROBIC UNIT controlled the amount of resistance and speed with which this device could be used to meet the variety of different exercise needs of our bodies.

The proper use of the Isorobic exercise unit combined the best features of Isometrics, Isotonics, Isokinetics and Aerobic Exercise. To explain why each of these are essential to us, I will call a little "time out" right here to explain these principles.

An ISOMETRIC exercise is a static contraction of the muscle. You can pull or push while tightening your muscle, thus building up strength very quickly. Ten seconds is the optimal time for benefitting from this exercise. When Isometrics became the rage, the average American got a little too carried away with the simplicity of it all. He would say, "Hey, here's the answer to my problem. All I'm going to have to do is get up every morning, tighten every muscle in my body for ten seconds, run over, take a shower, and I'm done." This sounded great, but unfortunately, it doesn't work out that way.

While it is true that you can build up strength in such a fashion, you are doing nothing for your heart, lungs, and arteries. Isometric exercise does not help flexibility or muscle balance. It only builds up brute strength in the particular area in which it is being used.

ISOTONIC exercise means exercise with movement. One of the objectives of exercise with movement is fatigue which is possible with repetitive isotonic exercise. Fatigue can be hastened with the use of weights. When I was in high school, the coach always warned us against the use of weights. "You'll be able to lift barbells and not be able to scratch the back of your neck," he advised us.

Certainly this is an exaggeration, but it does underline the difficulty connected with leverage. It takes more strength to get things moving than to keep them moving. The value of the weight lifting changes dramatically according to the leverage or angle from gravity in which we position our bodies.

ISOKENETIC exercise allows for the variations in our leverage angle by controlling resistance and speed. This allows for complete exercise of the muscles rather than just those called into play in traditional weight lifting exercises. The muscle works consistently through the entire range of motion. Nowadays, major gymnasiums have very expensive equipment to allow members this maximum advantage of their exercise efforts.

AEROBICS is the form of exercise that is now very popular. Basically, it is fast activity, sometimes dancing, which causes the heart, lungs and arteries to work hard. Aerobics stimulate the heart rate and heart pressure. The goal is working until the rate of heart beat has been raised sufficiently to create a conditioning effect on the heart muscle.

For a person to be totally fit, he or she must have all of these forms of exercise. It is not enough for a person to look fit. Recently a man who had just won one of those "body-beautiful contests" failed the Seattle police examinations because he could not get on and off a chair for three minutes. Everyone knows stories of people who have just walked out from a medical examination where they were pronounced in the best of health, only to drop dead of a heart attack.

Three Days and Seventy-Nine Orders

By the conclusion of the Isorobic exercise system demonstration at the football clinic, I had become a true believer. I saw that the advantages of this device went far beyond just my team's performance, or my own well-being. I couldn't wait to get back to school and demonstrate it for my football players. I showed it to everybody and anybody. This marvelous little device, weighing less than two pounds, integrated the best qualities of ISOMET-RICS, ISOTONICS, ISOKINETICS, AND AERO-BICS!

I, who was once so reluctant to even admit to myself that I had a problem, was now shouting to the world that I had an answer! Within three days, I had seventy-nine orders for the Isorobic Exercise System and I wasn't even selling them! Imagine the surprise of the demonstrators when I showed up on their doorstep. I was immediately invited to work as a consultant with the designers of the unit who used it with the Apollo Space Program.

What was so appealing to me is that I could use the system for only six to fifteen minutes a day and get a total workout. This certainly was the solution I had been desperately looking for. I soon realized I had reprioritized my life. Happiness to me is God first;   then   health, family and job. Without health, none of us would be able to have family or job for very long.

Helping Others

My discovery of the ISOROBIC EXERCISE SYS-TEM expanded my horizons. Before, my interest was basically just helping my players and students. After that one football clinic, I was interested in everybody's fitness.

My involvement as a consultant opened many

new doors. I found it a real honor to participate in research for our space program. We found out important factors related to inactivity and were able to take measures to prevent these stresses from occuring in the cramped confines of the space capsule. I have now worked with a wide range of famous athletes, football players, basketball players, hockey players and runners. I have had the pleasure of observing their remarkable advances in strength and flexibility through the use of the ISOROBIC EXERCISE UNIT. My greatest satisfaction probably comes from helping average individuals whose own situations are similar to the one that I confronted when I faced my mirror that fateful New Year's Day so long ago.

I now weigh 183 pounds and can do things far superior to what I could do at the age of 25; this includes running a six-minute mile! I am happier than I ever was before, because now I realize how fitness and happiness go hand in hand. I tour the country telling people they will be happy when they look good, feel good, and are physically fit.

I serve as a living example of the positive power of physical fitness, and how to achieve it.

To do more for the world than the world does for you
— that is success.   - Henry Ford

DAVID B. BRIZIUS
251 Cotswold Place
Gahanna, Ohio 43230
(614) 471-1141

David B. Brizius, C.S.P.

David B. Brizius is a nationally known sales trainer, motivational speaker, and advertising executive, who is also a professional magician. He uses his magic to demonstrate meaningful parts of his talks. Under the general title of "Magic With a Message" he has many programs, such as "The Magic of Advertising," "The Magic of Selling," and others. He has been honored by the National Speakers Associaton with the C.S.P. designation. (Certified Speaking Professional)

As Corporate Director of Marketing Communication for Copco Papers Inc., one of America's largest paper merchants, Mr. Brizius is in charge of Corporate Public Relations, Advertising, Sales Promotion and Sales Training. He has written a sales training program called TNT. His experience covers everything from retail sales, to manufacturing, to distribution.

In addition to his position with Copco Papers, Dave heads his own company, "Magi-Promotions" which provides clients with a variety of services: Sales Training, Magic with a Message Programs (1/2 hr to 3 days) Incentive Travel Programs, Advertising, Sales Promotion, and Magic Shows.

Dave is Past Chairman of Education and Training for the National Paper Trade Association. He serves on advisory committees for Advertising and Sales Promotion for some of America's leading paper mills. He is Past President of the Columbus Ohio Advertising Federation, and as such served on the Board of Directors of the Columbus Chamber of Commerce. (Ex-officio)

Since 1956 Dave and his wife Janice have directed an Interfaith, Interracial Church Camp which Parents Magazine chose as one of the "best youth programs in the United States." The Brizius' have been honored by two of Ohio's Governors with the Award for Community Service.

The Brizius' are also owners of the Magic Waters Theater, an Ohio summer theater which features Broadway shows under the stars.

Only You Can Be a Mover, Shaker, or a Change Maker
"The Magic of Selling is You"

By David B. Brizius

*"Oh Lord, Thou givest us everything,
at the price of an effort."*
- Leonardo Da Vinci

When you read the words, "The Magic of Selling," you may be thinking to yourself, "Oh brother, here's another dreamer offering some pie-in-the-sky formula for instant success. Indeed, the term

"The Magic of" has become an overused and exaggerated expression. However, when I talk about "The Magic of Selling," I really am talking about the magic which I include in my presentations.

A professional magician before I became a salesman, it was a natural transition to put a little magic into my sales presentations. It has become (excuse the pun) my gimmick. I do small magic (close-up) tricks for my customers. Many times I give away magic tricks as customer gifts.

Perhaps you would like to make magic your sales gimmick. "Too hard," you think, "Too much work." Well, at the risk of diminishing my reputation, let me tell you, it's not actually all that hard. You would be amazed at how easy doing magic really is.

I mentioned before that magic is my "gimmick." I think it is important for everyone in sales to have a gimmick. No it doesn't have to be magic. Certainly magic would not be suited to everyone. However, there are many other gimmicks you may use. Ideally your gimmick should be uniquely YOU.

The great speaker, Joel Weldon says, "Find out what everyone else is doing— then do something else." In this copy-cat world we live in, that is certainly good advice, and most appropriate in choosing your gimmick.

What are some other things you could do? Well, as I said before, I would prefer you select an idea of your own, however, here are a few things that salespeople I know use as gimmicks:

-One salesman always wears a fresh carnation in his lapel.

-One uses several different styles of business cards, and even has these cards printed on six different colors of paper.

-One always brings gifts, advertising specialties, etc.

-Another brings candy and keeps a candy bowl in the lobby full. (He also provided the candy bowl)

-One salesperson brings donuts for breakfast.

You see, there is no limit of gimmicks you can use to be unique, to make you just a little bit special in the minds of your customers. A gimmick may get you in the door, and it may make your customers remember you. However, it really is going to be your selling skills that make you the super salesperson you would like to be.

Some Selling Magic You Can Use TODAY! The Magic of the Competitor Profile

This next bit of magic requires you to use a pen or pencil as opposed to a magic wand.

I hope that you understand that it takes time to perfect and then use a selling skill. Just like anything else, you can't become an expert in a day. However, in this chapter I would like to show you something that can be used immediately.

Some years ago my company sent me to attend a very famous, expensive and excellent two and one half day sales seminar. A short time later

I found myself going all over the country presenting this same seminar for others. This particular course taught "The Four Factors for Successful Selling" which are:

1. Product Knowledge
2. Company Knowledge
3. Customer Knowledge
4. Selling Skills

Soon after I began teaching this course, I realized that there was a necessary 5th factor for successful selling: COMPETITOR KNOWLEDGE.

Yes, you must know your competition, and I am pleased to present what I call the "Competitor Profile" which you will find on the following page. You can see from the example that we list our top three or four competitors in order.

Since we're in the people business, we'll first list our competition by the name of the salesperson. Second, we list our competitor's strong points. What is it that makes this person so good? Indeed, if your competitor is doing something well, you may want to do it too. Next you will list your competitor's weaknesses. Finally comes the most important part: You develop a plan, and PUT IT IN WRITING to BEAT YOUR COMPETITION!

Indeed, your competition will probably change from account to account, so you may want to fill out several of these competitor profiles. Granted, this takes a little time, but it is time well spent. As you become more sophisticated in your competitor analylsis, you may wish to add these things to your competitor profile:

Shipping Point or Office: _____

Area Served from Office: _____

Size of Warehouse: _____

Number of Employees: _____

Comments from Customers: _____

COMPETITOR PROFILE

COMPETITOR (Person's Name): _____

STRENGTHS: _____

WEAKNESSES: _____

_____

A PLAN TO "BEAT THE COMPETITION" (Person's Name): _____

_____

_____

COMPETITOR (Person's Name): _____

STRENGTHS: _____

_____

WEAKNESSES: _____

_____

A PLAN TO "BEAT THE COMPETITION" (Person's Name): _____

_____

It is very important for a salesperson to keep good records, and the competitor profile should be a part of those records. A couple of times a year you may wish to re-evaluate lead positions. The reason a particular competitor is doing so well with one of your customers may give you a good clue as to what and how to promote for your next order. PLEASE REALIZE THAT THIS IS SOMETHING YOU CAN START ON TODAY.

I really believe that this COMPETITOR PRO-FILE will be a help to you. However, without the other four factors for successful selling, you probably still won't become that super salesperson you want to be. Let's go over these important ideas.

The Magic of Product Knowledge

Too often people don't get the sale because they lack a thorough knowledge of their product or service. These unsuccessful salespeople particularly have trouble relating their product knowledge to their benefits. This could be because people have trouble distinguishing between FEATURES and BENEFITS.

The American Heritage Dictionary defines BENEFIT as "Anything that promotes or enhances well-being: advantage." Your customer simplifies that. He or she says, "What's in it for me?"

Webster's New World Dictionary defines FEATURE as a "distinct or outstanding part, quality, or characteristic of something." A feature means nothing except as it relates to your customer's needs.

If your sales presentation uses only features, not benefits, it likely won't relate to your prospect. Remember, your customers always look for benefits, (not features) and always say, **"What's in it for me?"**

Perhaps you are still unsure of the difference between a feature and a benefit. Let's see if we can't clear that up. Below are listed some of the features and benefits of a new car:

Feature	Benefit
Reclining Seats	Passengers can be comfortable and arrive refreshed, maybe even take a nap on the way.
Rear Window Defrost	No scraping on cold mornings; keeps rear window clear of snow and fog while traveling.
Air Conditioning	Passengers can be cool and comfortable, and not be "blown away" by open windows.
DeLuxe Interior	Makes the driver feel important, prestigious.
Cruise Control	Gas savings; more comfortable driving; can eliminate "lead-footing" and getting a speeding ticket.
Side Mirrors	Ease in passing, watching surrounding traffic.

I'm sure you can think of even better examples now that you understand the difference.

With the fast changes taking place in products today, it is especially important to be up to date on your product knowledge. In my business, the printing and industrial paper industry, at least one new product or major product improvement is announced weekly. You cannot have too much product knowledge, especially as it relates to your customers' needs.

The Magic of Company Knowledge

How well do you know your company? In seminars I have jokingly suggested that company knowledge means more than knowing how many weeks of vacation you have. Does your company have credit policies? Returned goods policies? Entertainment policies? Let's take this one step further: What are your company's capabilities when it comes to service, delivery and production? It would be a serious mistake on your part if you were to ask your customers questions about their service needs if you couldn't deliver.

The Magic of Customer Knowledge

Good sales managers often say, "Love those customers!" And you know, they're right, for without the customers we have no income or future sales.
A major problem for many sales people is that they take customers for granted. Just because a certain customer has always bought your product or service from you does not

mean that they always will. Your steady customers deserve as much attention as your prospective ones. YOU MUST SATISFY CUSTOMER NEEDS.

This is tricky— you'll need to pay close attention! Your product or service may have benefits that you feel are important, but it is only when you satisfy the NEEDS OF YOUR CUSTOMER with the BENEFITS THAT MEET THOSE NEEDS that you will get an order. Too often salespeople talk about features and benefits that don't meet their customers' needs, and they lose the sale.

Do some research. Find out what your customers' needs are. With a little luck you'll find a benefit to meet those needs. Now you have something to present to them.

If you have been calling on the same customers for a long time, you might think customer knowledge of them would be a snap. This is not necessarily the case. Customers' needs are constantly changing. Are you keeping up with those changes? Could your competiton be getting more and more business by way of the "back door" while you are just standing around at the "front door"? Are you leaving too much business "on the table?"

The first and foremost thing you must know about your customer is what person or persons make the buying decisions. As you acquire more and more information on a particular account, you may find that there are people in various other departments or divisions who do their own buying. You need to get to know these people.

What happens when your customer hires new people, or changes ownership? Since you will not have a rapport with these new people, you'd better take time to develop a relationship.

Is a key prospect expanding or setting new goals and directions? Keeping in touch definitely relates to customer knowledge. For a cold call, or in an old established climate, there are ways to determine what's going on. The best way, of course, is to ask good questions. Talking with the receptionist, listening to other sales people, reading the newspaper and your on-call observations are all good ways of getting leads on customer knowledge.

A SALE IS NOT A SALE UNTIL THE BILL IS PAID. Too often, an old reliable well-paying account goes out of business or "bellies up" as we say. You must constantly be on the look-out for signs that your customer is in financial trouble. These are some things you might observe:

-Excessive turn-over of personnel.

-Deteriorating office decor.

-An offer to give you business that has previously been a competitor's.

-They miss taking discounts for prompt payment.

-They elongate the days outstanding on their unpaid balance.

Naturally your credit manager will be aware of these last two items. However, as a good sales person, regardless of how much you want a sale, be sure to alert your credit manager to these other subtle changes.

The Magic of Selling Skills

Professional selling is more than having a big smile and an outgoing personality. It is using skills to help your customer make the buying decision that is best for him. I highly recommend that you enroll in one of the many outstanding programs that will teach you methods of selling by overcoming objections, skepticism, and the ever-present indifference. Attending one of these programs will definitely put money in your pocket.

Let me, today, give you some skills that probably aren't covered by the above-mentioned programs.

1. YOU WILL HAVE 10 SECONDS OF UNDIVIDED ATTENTION EVERY TIME YOU USE YOUR CUSTOMER'S NAME. If, while making a sales call your prospect listens and understands every word you say, this first selling skill won't help much. On the other hand, if the buyer is distracted by the many activities that go on in an office, you might try this technique: "So you see, Mr. Smith, this particular product might be just what you've been looking for."

2. CAREFULLY PRE-PLAN YOUR SALES CALL and set a call objective. When you close, you close to achieve that *call objective.* Your call objective may not be to make a sale, but rather to do such things as *set up a test, or trial program, arrange to make a presentation to a committee, set up a survey, make a plant tour, etc.*

3. THE MAGIC WORDS IN SELLING: 'OH, WHY NOT?" Whenever your close is turned down, do not shut your briefcase and leave, but rather use what I call the MAGIC WORDS OF SELLING. **'Oh why not?"** When you ask this question there is a very good chance that you will be told the circumstances you face. Your customer will probably actually tell you the obstacles you must overcome to make the sale. GO FOR IT!

So Where's The Magic?

Perhaps you've decided that all this sounds like a lot of hard work; not magic at all. Well, in a way that's right. No hokus-pokus will turn you into a super salesperson. But by perfecting these various areas we've discussed, it can indeed SEEM LIKE MAGIC.

As you learn to execute the "basic moves" of sales, your selling will become fun.

SELLING SHOULD BE FUN. It can be if you put a little magic into your presentation. Your "magic" will be the "special spark" you generate — your uniqueness. Remember to "find out what everyone else is doing, then do something else."

No one else can be you. Capitalize on that. Put some **PERSONALIZED MAGIC** into your selling.

JAMES L. SLOAN
Christian Singles International
Box 610
Zionsville, IN 46077
(3l7)769-5569

MEMBER

NATIONAL SPEAKERS ASSOCIATION

James L. Sloan

A checkerboard best describes the background of James L. Sloan. He majored in philosophy at the University of Missouri at Kansas City, but has also studied at Graceland College, Indiana University, and Purdue University.

His studies and his work have included everything from chemistry and pest control, business and entrepreneurship, to all the social sciences, including psychology, sociology, religion, and marriage and family counseling.

He has founded various types of businesses from Ohio to California as well as Canada. His last business venture was an ice cream vending operation which he took from zero to over 250 distributors and dealers within four years.

An ordained minister for l6 years, Jim has spent many years teaching classes to all age groups - in church, at church camps and retreats, and to different singles groups. He has also spent many hours in counseling people about personal and family problems; everything from alcohol and drug abuse to finances to health to relationships.

He has written and edited various motivational newsletters. He has been an officer of Optimist Clubs, Toastmasters Clubs, and Parents Without Partners.

Jim is currently executive director of Christian Singles International, an organization dedicated to helping singles achieve emotional stability and spiritual maturity by creating a proper relationship with God and Christ, and then with other people. He also edits their newsletter, "Your Christian Companion," which features inspirational, Christ centered articles plus Christian singles ads.

In addition, he conducts seminars and workshops on LEARNING TO LIVE ALONE WITHOUT BEING LONELY, RESOLVING PERSONAL CONFLICTS, CHOOSING THE RIGHT COMPANION, GETTING RIGHT WITH GOD - GETTING RIGHT WITH PEOPLE, etc. He will go anywhere, anytime, to help people have better
relationships.

Self-Discipline is the Road to Lasting Happiness

By James L.Sloan

"The undisciplined life is not worth living."
— Socrates
"And sorrow is turned into joy before God."
— Job 41:22

Over 90% of your mental conceptions at this moment are in error. And so are mine. Historically we know this is true. Think of some of your forefathers' beliefs:

Everything is made out of four "elements" — fire, air, earth and water.

The earth is flat. The sun revolves around the earth.

If a train were to go over 30 miles per hour, it would explode. (Early   1800's)

Man will never fly. (Late 1800's)

I could name many more and come right up to the present, but you get the idea. However, let's think about now. Let's think about you. Why can't you step into a phone booth in California, put in a coin, dial New York, and when the connection is made: Instead of talking to New York, BE in New York? There is only one reason. You can't visualize it. So it's impossible. But is this really any more impossible than airplanes or computers were 100 years ago?

Our Knowledge Is Imperfect

God created man in HIS image. How are we in God's image? Does God have two arms, two legs, etc. He hasn't told me, but I doubt it. We're in God's image in that we have a small portion of God's infinite intelligence. But our intelligence is finite, imperfect. So we now laugh at the things people "knew" 1000 years ago. The process of finding our "facts" outmoded is speeding up all the time.

Because of this increasingly rapid pace of knowledge obsolescence, most of us today know that we don't really know very much. We know that what we **know** today as truth will be false tomorrow. At least subconsciously we know this. We read or hear almost daily of some cherished concept that is now known to be false. It happens in medicine and health, in space, in the earth's composition. But it's not just in the physical realm that so much of our "knowledge" is incorrect.

Our knowledge explosion is creating havoc with human relationships. Look at the appalling statistics on crime, abortion, divorce, child abuse. Our exploding knowledge has a close correlation with the explosions that are going on in families. We seem to know more and more facts every year and know less and less about how to cope. People find it hard to cope with each other, with "the system,' with themselves. People are alienated from each other and from God.

Faulty Knowledge - Faulty Relationships

Why do over 50% of all marriages now end in divorce? Is being married and having a traditional family good or is it not? If not, why do most of us still want to get married— and to "that special someone"? If it is good, why do most marriages fail? And there are even more failed marriages than the statistics indicate— people that just don't bother to get a divorce even though they no longer live together; people that stay together for the kids; for appearances; or from sheer inertia.

At Christian Singles International, we believe in marriage. Which may seem like a contradiction to you. It's not. We accept the world as it is today — which is all mixed up! It is the very fact of the world (which is people) being confused which makes Christian Singles International possible— and viable. There are millions of people that are alone but do not want to be alone— yet are not satisfied with the casualness of today's mores. Christian Singles International is God and Christ centered. All of our teachings are based on the Bible.

In Genesis 2:23-24 we find, "And I, the Lord God, said that it was not good that the man should be alone. Wherefore, I will make an help meet for him." Skipping down to verse 30 it says, "Therefore shall a man leave his father and mother, and shall cleave unto his wife; and they shall be one flesh." That's the way the Bible says it **should** be. But seldom is it so today. People try (sometimes desperately so) to work on the part about "not being alone." We anxiously try to find someone to marry so we won't be alone. Or most of us who aren't looking for a marriage partner are looking for someone to live with — for years, months, or at least for the night.

That solves the "being alone" part. But what about verse 30? "And they shall be one flesh." Being one flesh doesn't mean having physical sex. Ephesians 5:28 says, "So ought men to love their wives as their own bodies. He that loves his wife loves himself. For no man ever yet hated his own flesh, but nourishes it and cherishes it." To be of one flesh we have to accept the other person AS IS.

Long nose or short nose. Fat or skinny. Tall or short.

Complete Acceptance Necessary

But the acceptance has to be in everything — not just the physically obvious. Does he snore? Learn to love it. Does she giggle on the phone like a teenager? Learn to love it. Does he have weird friends? Don't try to avoid them. Find out what he likes about them and learn to love them. Does she only wash a dish when the cabinets are empty and the dishes are piled high in the sink? Learn to understand why— and in the process watch your love for her grow. WHATEVER the characteristics of your partner — however strange or zany it may seem to you at first, learn to accept the whole person — AS IS. This is the **only** way your love can grow. This is the **only** way you can become one flesh.

Few of us do this. So, even when we think we have solved the problem of "being alone," we're still lonely. What is the difference between "being alone" and "lonely"? The dictionary says:

ALONE, not with others; without the help of others.

LONELY, sad because one lacks friends or companions.

LONELY HEART, one who feels permanently lonely.

To be alone is neither good nor bad. It is

simply the physical state a person is in. To be lonely, though, can be terrible. It is a mental state. Depending on your personal mental and emotional condition, it can affect you a little or a lot. You are mildly anxious because your child is 15 minutes late from school. Or you are horrified because your husband has just announced he is in love with his secretary.

The amount of trauma you experience is NOT determined by the condition. Your trauma comes from your **perception** of the condition.

Fact: Your child is 15 minutes late.

Your Perception: A. He's been kidnapped. (Very unlikely, but if you keep thinking about it, you will be hysterical in a few more minutes.) B. He stopped to play with the boy down the street. (Much more likely.)

Fact: Your husband is infatuated with his secretary.

Your Perception: A. You are disgraced. You can't face your neighbors or see your friends in church. Maybe you should commit suicide or murder or at least kick him out. B. Perhaps I haven't been showing him I love him as much as I really do. Maybe if I work at letting him know I really love him, this will blow over and our marriage will be better than ever.

Granted, I have used extreme examples. The point is that all emotions are internal, not external. Loneliness is no exception. An emotionally distraught person will go into hysterics on a small, routine external event. An emotionally stable person may remain calm while the walls are caving in.

Alone, But Not Lonely

I live alone, but I am not lonely. I live alone because my wife chooses to live elsewhere. I love her; I miss her; and I would prefer that she come home. But until such time as she decides to come back, I am alone. Yet, I am not alone. God is with me and strengthens me every day, hence loneliness is not part of my life.

This was not always the case. For months before she left we didn't really communicate. We talked. I tried and she tried; but it was like one of us was speaking French and the other Japanese. Although we were together I was very lonely (and so was she, I think).

When she actually moved out of the house I **truly** discovered loneliness! I would see the anniversary certificate she had given me from "The Society of Splendid Spouses" hanging on my office wall. Or the collection of family photographs on the living room wall. Or the beautiful canopy cover and bedspread she had made for our bed.

I tried to work and keep occupied; but wasn't very productive. I would wander around the house at night realizing how good it could have been if I hadn't loused it up. In my frustration I wanted to drive my fist through a wall. I wanted to explode but couldn't. A rumbling volcano that couldn't erupt.

That's loneliness That's hell on earth.

Because we are lonely, we tend to try to find someone else to cure our problem. It won't work. When two lonely people find each other, they are no longer alone. But being with someone does not necessarily solve the loneliness problem.

Learn To Live Alone

The only real cure for loneliness is to learn to live alone! No one else can cure loneliness for you. You have to learn to live with yourself and love yourself. Until you love yourself, you're not going to get much love from anyone else. Until you love yourself, you definitely don't have any excess love to share with others.

In John 16:32, Jesus said, "And they shall leave me alone; and yet I am not alone, because the Father is with me." It was only by reading scriptures such as these that my loneliness began to leave. There are dozens more. If you are lonely today, you need to search the Bible for them. Don't spend all your time trying to find another person to cure your loneliness for you. Rather, spend your time in learning to live alone − learning to live without being lonely.

You may not be able to change the external circumstances − whether you are alone because your spouse died, alone after a divorce, alone from never having married, or even if you are "alone" in a poor marriage. But you CAN change the inside of **you**. You can change the way you see the situation.

How do you change your perception? How do you learn to live alone without being lonely? You have to become acquainted with a word we don't like in our permissive society today — DISCIPLINE. The world says, "Do your own thing. Live however you want. It doesn't make any difference to anyone else. Nobody cares how you act or what you do."

The world's way is seldom true — just expedient. This is no exception. Let's check the wisdom of Solomon. Proverbs 1:7,10, "The fear of the Lord is the beginning of knowledge; but fools despise wisdom and instruction. If sinners entice you, do not consent." Chapter 5, verses 22 & 23, "And he shall be held with the cords of his sins. He shall die without instruction; and in the greatness of his folly he shall go astray" The virtue of discipline is all through the book. Look at 6:6-9, "Go to the ant, you sluggard; consider its way, and be wise; which having no overseer or ruler, provides its meat in the summer and gathers its food in the harvest. How long will you sleep, you sluggard? When will you wake up." There's lots more all through the book of Proverbs. If you want to learn discipline, study the book of Proverbs.

Is Solomon too pious for you? We can start in a completely different way and end up at the same place. Socrates said, "The undisciplined life is not worth living." Socrates or Solomon, Religious or secular, the conclusion is the same. Discipline is the beginning of a satisfactory life.

And it's still true as we near the 21st century. Napoleon Hill said, "While others may sidetrack you, remember that discouragement most frequently comes from within." "You have the power to control your thoughts." and "Self control is merely thought control."

We often think of discipline as punishment. But that is only meaning number three in the dictionary. The **first** meaning of discipline is, "training that produces obedience, self control, or a particular skill." A synonym for discipline is orderliness. Is your life out of order? The beginning of getting it in order is self-discipline.

Is Disaster Necessary To Learn?

Do we have to learn self-discipline in health and fitness by getting sick? Do we have to learn self-discipline in human relationships by going through 16 divorces or affairs? Do we have to learn self-discipline in our finances by going bankrupt? Unfortunately, this is the only way some of us learn. And some never learn. I have to admit I am a slow learner. I sometimes feel that God has to bang me on the head with a hammer a few times before I get the message. I'm 53 years old and just beginning to really learn.

But **you** could take a shortcut. You could make a conscious decision— right now— that you are going to make self-discipline a part of your life. I carry a little card in my pocket at all times. It says:

"Right and wrong are discernible. Doing what is right, even though difficult, is always the best possible course of action. Doing what is right is always right."

Discipline Leads To Joy

Deciding that you want order in your life is one thing. Exercising the discipline to get the job done is something else. How many New Year's resolutions have you kept past January 15th? You may need a little help. Here are three things I do first thing every morning to help me remember to exercise self-discipline in my life all day:

1. I make my bed. This may sound simple to you neatniks and silly to you clutterbugs. But as I make the bed I think **why** I am making it— to put my mind in the mode of self-discipline for the day.

2. I get on my rowing machine. I had the contraption over three years before I used it consistently. About every 90 days I would say, "I've got to get in shape." I'd start a religious rowing program that would last 10 days or two weeks.

Finally, I found a way to trick myself. I parked the machine in front of my dresser! I can't get to my socks and shorts without moving the rowing machine. That got me past the barrier. I still keep it in front of the dresser, but it doesn't matter anymore. I never miss.

And I won't. I'm currently doing about seven times as many strokes as I could when I started. What was hard — and took lots of self-discipline — is now easy. I have made it into a habit.

3. I shave. For over nine years straight I wore a beard. I always told folks the reason for the beard was to save time — five minutes trimming once a week instead of five minutes daily shaving. 1/2 hour a week saved = 26 hours a year. The the real reason was: I JUST DON'T LIKE TO SHAVE!

So now I shave to add self-discipline to my life. After nine years of **not** shaving, with every stroke of the razor I think about **WHY** I am doing it. I am shaving to set the pattern of self-discipline for the day.

I don't care whether **you** make your bed, use a rowing machine, or shave (or whatever ladies do instead). These are things that work for me. You need to find whatever works for you.

Gift of Choice

The greatest gift God gave you is your intelligence— it's imperfect, but nevertheless part of His perfect intelligence. His second greatest gift to you is your right of choice. You weren't created as a robot. You can choose where you want to live, how you want to live. Whether you want to eat nutritious food or junk. Whether you want to be giving or selfish. Most of all, whether you want to think positively or negatively— good or evil.

But there's a catch to the gift. You HAVE to stand by your choices. If you jump off a cliff, you're going to crash. If you jump off a mental or spiritual cliff by thinking negative or evil thoughts, you're going to crash.

If you want good things to start happening in your life (external), you need to start putting some good thoughts into your head (internal). More of Solomon's wisdom, "As a man thinketh in his heart, so is he." The first— and hardest —discipline you need to work on, is disciplining your own thoughts.

You have to get right in your head before you can ever get anything else right— your environment or your relationships. And only **you** can to it. No one else can do it for you. Nevertheless, the goal of Christian Singles International is to create an environment that helps people to come closer to God and to develop their God given talents to their maximum potential. We do this by helping singles achieve emotional stability and spiritual maturity through seminars, workshops, local chapter meetings, "Your Christian Companion" newsletter, books and other motivational materials.

Many single people spend a lot of time searching for a mate. And naturally we want it to be "Mr. Right" or "Miss Perfect." But rarely is Miss Perfect or Mr. Right found. People search in all the wrong places— bars, singles parties or dances, singles newspapers, etc. The place to begin the search is in your head. Soul-searching rather than body searching.

Work On Yourself

Concentrate on improving yourself instead of finding a perfect person. An amazing thing will happen if you do this. As you make yourself better and better, you will be putting yourself into a win-win mode. (A) You have a much better chance of attracting someone who is "worthy of you." Or (B) If not, you will still feel a lot better about yourself. Back to my rowing machine, for example. I don't always **want** to get on the thing every morning. But if I feel terrible, I row anyway. When I finish rowing I **always** feel good. Another victory!

Whenever you exercise, you get two rewards. First, your own health is improved (emotional health, too). Second, you have become a slightly better "catch" for someone of the other sex through your own better health.

This is true in all five areas of life— spiritual, mental, physical, social, and financial. Are you working on your growth in all five areas? If not, you are dying. In the whole universe everything is either growing, dying, or dead. Including the Sun, the Earth, and You. I would not want to live with a dead person. Would you? Dead things stink. YOU don't want to stink. So come alive. You can come alive by working at **growing** in all these five areas of your life. And you **do** need all five for balance. You can be a millionaire **financially** and die of cancer at 50 because **mentally** you couldn't quit smoking. So what good did the money do? You could be in perfect **physical** health through good eating and exercise habits; but have no friends because you have never been able to get your spiritual and social self together. So what good is that perfect body?

Christian Singles International has a booklet available that will help you with all five areas in your life. It's called, "Balancing on Life's Tightrope - Even If You Don't Have a Safety Net." If you would like information, write to Box 610, Zionsville, IN 46077.

When you have learned to live alone, when you have conquered your own loneliness, then you are ready for the possibility of uniting your life with someone else. As you are growing, so are many other people. There are many people in the world that you could **choose** to love. What you DON'T want to do is **fall** in love. That's dangerous. Who wants to fall into anything? And if you **fall** in love, later on you may **fall out** of love. It's not worth it.

There is no security in "falling in love." The only real question if you do is— who will fall out first, you or your partner?

Creating a Perfect Union

Since our knowledge is always less than perfect,

how can you **ever** KNOW enough about your prospective partner to be sure it will last? It's impossible. To prove for yourself that the world's way of seeking after knowledge will not work, all you have to do is look at the marriage and divorce statistics.

The only way that has any semblance of a guarantee is through proper relationships. That starts by having a solid relationship with God. Your **only** security begins here— with God.

When two people each have a proper relationship with God, then they have a chance at having a good relationship with each other. Two people can **choose** to anchor together for eternity. Two people can **choose** to believe in each other. Your trust in each other must be based on faith — not knowledge. You can never know enough to trust him/her. But if you have faith in God, then in each other, perfect trust will come.

The only way to have perfect security is to establish solid relationships — through faith.

Are you now in a marriage with this kind of an ideal relationship? If so, marvelous!

If you are now in a marriage and one or both of you have not made that 100% commitment, hopefully this article has helped. If you would like more help, contact us at Christian Singles International. You CAN choose to make your marriage work!

If you are now living alone, may we invite you to join C.S.I.? If you believe in God and believe that God has a purpose for the world and for you;

Christian Singles International offers you fellowship with others who think the same. People that are trying to improve their lives day by day.

"Ask and you shall receive, that your joy might be full.

-John 16:24

Life is not a having and a getting, but a being and becoming.

- Matthew Arnold

MARGE HIDALGO
311 Longview Rd.
Waukegan, IL 60087
(312) 623-9661

Marge Hidalgo

Marge Hidalgo is Co-Owner (with her husband Carlos) of Hidalgo Management, a property management firm. Born and raised in Oak Park, Illinois, Marge attended Radcliffe College in Cambridge, Mass., for 2 years and graduated from Northwestern University with a B.S. in Romance Languages.

Marge and her husband have lived on 4 continents and visited more than 50 countries. Their interests include photography (producing 3-screen, 9 projector slide shows), boating and computers. They currently live in Waukegan, Illinois and have two daughters, Laura and Sandra, and one grandson, Harrison.

Marge is a member of the National Speakers Association, Toastmasters and Women in Management.

Her purpose is to help others raise their financial consciousness (particularly women) with her Prosperity Workshop, "10 Steps to a Million Dollars." Marge also is certified by the American-International Reiki Association, Inc. to teach The Radiance Technique (sm): The Official Reiki Program ®, a very powerful self-help technique for stress reduction, positive wellness and personal growth.

TEN STEPS TO A MILLION DOLLARS:
How to Become Financially Independent

By Marge Hidalgo

*"A small daily task, if it be really daily,
will beat the labours of a spasmodic Hercules."*
— Anthony Trollope

In 1960 while browsing at my favorite bookstore, I picked up a book with an intriguing title: "How I Turned $1,000 into $1,000,000 in Real Estate in my Spare Time," by William Nickerson. I brought it home to share it with my husband Carlos, not realizing how this book would completely change our lives.

We had been married in December, 1950 after we both graduated from college. I received my B.S. degree from Northwestern University in Romance Languages and Carlos got his degree in Mechanical Engineering from Illinois Institute of Technology. At the time we were married, our big dream was to travel and live overseas.

Carlos went to work for the international department of a manufacturer of heating and air conditioning equipment, and I got a job with the United Nations. Our first overseas post was Lima, Peru, where our daughter Laura was born. We returned to the U.S. and in 1953 Carlos came home one evening and asked, "How would you like to go to the Belgian Congo?" I didn't even know where the Belgian Congo was! I went to the New York Public Library the next day to find out more about this Central African country. There wasn't too much information available, but it was considered a hardship post by the U.S. Government.

We had been hoping to be sent to either Europe or South America. One redeeming feature about the Belgian Congo (now Zaire) was that to get there, you had to go through Europe or South America. Because it was a hardship post, at the end of two years we received a four month vacation plus first class travel allowance to the United States. There were no travel agents in Leopoldville (now Kinshasa), so I did all the planning and arrangements for a four month trip to South America, the United States and Europe.

I found that I loved doing the research necessary to plan an extended trip. We learned that we enjoyed independent travel, using the public transportation of the countries we visited and shopping and eating where the locals shopped and ate. Our first major purchase after we married was a 35 mm. camera, and we combined our interest in photography with our travels. The slide shows on Europe, Africa and South America that we presented to audiences in the United States were the beginning of an interest in public speaking.

We came back to the United States in 1956 to settle down and raise our family. By then my husband had decided that he no longer wanted to work for a big corporation. He got a job with a heating and air conditioning contractor in Waukegan, Illinois and completed the requirements for a Professional Engineer's license. In 1960, the contractor moved his business out of town and my husband hung out his shingle as a Consulting Engineer.

Financial Blueprint

Then William Nickerson's book entered our life. The book provided us with a blueprint to financial independence. We read it and re-read it, and made the commitment to become financially independent.

Sufficient independent income to meet our basic needs seemed like a glorious dream. We would be able to pursue the activities we really enjoyed, but which didn't offer much hope of making us wealthy.

While Carlos nurtured his fledgling Consulting Engineering practice, I started to shop for our first investment property. For six months, I spent several days each week looking at prospective investments. When I started, I had no idea of the comparative value of different properties. I learned that shopping for real estate wasn't any different than shopping for groceries or clothing. Anyone can become an expert who is willing to put in the time and look at enough properties.

Our first purchase was a two-bedroom house on 3/4 acre of land that was advertised in our local newspaper. The selling price was $5,500. We drove by the house, liked its looks, wrote out a crude offer-to-purchase and gave the owner a $100 deposit. After cleaning and painting the interior, installing new tile floors and adding a garage, we sold the house for $9,800 and were on our way! Before we sold the house, however, I spent many restless nights worrying about how we could continue to make the mortgage payments if we didn't find a tenant or buyer. I was beginning to learn to live with debt.

The next property we bought was a three unit apartment building for $6,300. The building had been condemned by the city and we were planning to tear it down. Our lawyer suggested that we renovate it instead. When we went inside we found thousands of cockroaches, so we called the exterminators. They refused to fumigate until we cleaned out the interior. Fortunately, the three years we had spent in Africa had increased my tolerance to bugs, but hauling trash out of that building was one of the unforgettable experiences of our investment career. It was also a test of our commitment to a long term goal. Our theme song that day could have been "What I Did For Love" from the show, Chorus Line.

Six months later, with a new heating system, new wiring, a new roof and painted inside and out, the three apartments rented quickly. By then it was clear we had found the right investment medium for us— one that was challenging, rewarding, used our skills, and was fun.

Five years later we owned 32 rental units and Carlos gave up his Consulting Engineering practice to join me as a full time real estate investor. From 1965 on, all of our income came from our investments. We had reached our goal of financial independence.

Our office was in our home and we enjoyed the freedom of not having to make the daily commute. I could do my paperwork at any hour of the day or night. However, we were also on call twenty four hours a day or night. At first we did as much of the maintenance work possible ourselves. This could mean going out at 2 a.m. on a frigid winter night to take care of a broken pipe or no-heat call. Over a period of many years, we learned to cope with every

possible variety of problems — human and mechanical, as well as natural disasters.

We continued buying properties until we
owned 200 rental units. Ten years later in 1975,
when we celebrated our Silver Wedding Anniversary, our net worth reached $1,000,000. Carlos'
response was, "Yes, and think of all the fun we've
had along the way."

Becoming a real estate investor gave me an
invaluable financial education. I learned to deal
with lawyers, accountants, contractors, bankers,
real estate brokers, and tenants. I learned a new
language — the language of money. It was rare for
me to meet another woman doing the same things
that I was. I wanted to motivate other women to
take control of their financial life, set goals and go
for it!

One day, a little voice inside said, "Marge, why
don't you teach a seminar on prosperity consciousness? You could call it "10 Steps to a Million
Dollars." Eventually this vision became a reality.

I'd like to share with you a few of the ideas that
I present in my workshop.

Wealth Begins on the Inside

You have to become wealthy inside before you can
become wealthy outside. Wealth and abundance
come from within and eventually manifest on the
outer planes. If you don't believe that you deserve
to prosper, guess what — chances are that you
never will.

Mike Todd, the producer of the movie,

"Around the World in Eighty Days" said, "I've been rich and I've been broke, but I've never been poor." Whatever his outward financial situation, he was wealthy inside.

Do you have permission to become wealthy? One way to find out is to work with affirmations. Take a sheet of paper and draw a line down the middle. On the left hand side write, "I deserve to prosper." Be still and listen to your inner voice. Write down whatever pops into your head. (It could be something like "Who are you kidding, you'll never amount to anything.")

You will gradually become aware of old beliefs and attitudes you are carrying around that may keep you from realizing your goal. Continue to write the affirmation and record whatever comes up. If you keep working with this technique you will begin to see a change in your responses. When you can write the affirmation, "I deserve to prosper," and your inner voice responds, "You certainly do!" your subsconscious will be working in harmony with your conscious mind to make your dreams a reality.

Change Your Poverty Consciousness to a Prosperity Consciousness

One of the ways you can increase your prosperity consciousness is to become aware of the abundance in your life right now!! You don't have to wait till you become a millionaire to enjoy most of life's pleasures. In fact, if you don't learn to enjoy life in the here-now, whatever your current financial status, chances are that no amount of money will ever bring you happiness.

Make a list of the little pleasures that enhance your life, and put it where you'll see it often. A walk in the park, watching the sunset, listening to a favorite record, soaking in a hot tub, or seeing a cardinal alight on the locust tree outside our dining room window, are some of the little things that add joy to my days.

A sense of humor and frequent belly laughs are also priceless. Did something make you smile today? Make a note of it in your journal. Observe the magnificent abundance of nature. Since abundance is the natural state of the universe, claim some of it as yours.

Pay Yourself First

A part of all you earn is yours to keep. I learned about this idea from a book entitled "The Richest Man in Babylon," by George S. Clason. According to this book, the First Law of Gold is that Gold cometh gladly and in increasing quantity to any man who will put by not less than one-tenth of his earnings to create an estate for his future and that of his family.

What can you do if you're spending up to the limit of your income now? You can freeze your current spending level and set aside any future raises for investment. You can also invest any unexpected windalls (gifts, income tax refunds, etc.). The sooner you begin a regular investment program, the sooner you will begin to take advantage of the miracle of the time-value of money.

If you start to work when you are 25 years old at a salary of $15,000, receive yearly raises of 4% and work for 35 years, you'll earn a total of $1,104,783. If you invest $100 per month for 35 years at 14% interest, you'll have $1,110,295 when you're ready to retire.

Developing the habit of "paying yourself first" and investing regularly for the long pull is definitely worth the effort! Do you really want to arrive at age sixty having earned over a million dollars, and wonder where it all went? As Thomas Gray said, "For all sad words of tongue or pen, the saddest are these: 'It might have been.'"

Keep Yourself Motivated

How can you overcome all the negative programming that you probably received along the way? Or keep going in the face of setbacks, discouragements, and downright disasters?

I use several tools to keep myself motivated. Some of these are affirmations, books, tapes, visual symbols and written goals.

A few years after we started our investment program, I was feeling depressed and sorry for myself because it was a few days before Christmas and there was little money available to buy presents for our two daughters. The roof on one of our buildings was leaking badly, and it seemed that we were not making any forward progress. My husband said he wanted to go to a toy store, but he wouldn't tell me what he was looking for. We drove all around town before he announced, "Mission accomplished." On Christmas Day when I opened my present, it was a miniature building kit. Carlos used it to construct our dream apartment building. This model had a prominent place in our living room for many years. Each day as I walked past it several times, it "spoke" to me and said, "Hold the dream, Marge."

Develop a Support Team

John Donne, a poet born in the sixteenth century, said, "No man is an island, entire of itself." It's just as true in the twentieth century. When we first came to Waukegan, we didn't know anyone. We found the best way to get to know people was to join groups and volunteer to work on a committee. We're still active in several organizations.

Many people helped us along the way — real estate brokers, contractors, lawyers, bankers, accountants. I was fortunate to work with a woman real estate broker. She sold us millions of dollars worth of real estate and also helped arrange financing. We made it a policy to be on a first-name basis with all the bank presidents in our community. Once a banker called us and asked if we could use some money (we seldom turn down an offer of this kind). We said "Sure," and with very little hassle refinanced a building with a new loan of several hundred thousand dollars. Another "What's new?" visit I made to a banker produced a lead to a valuable property that was being fore-closed. Later we purchased the property for a fraction of its real value in bankruptcy court.

You may know some members of your support team only through books or tapes. Napoleon Hill, author of "Think and Grow Rich," held imaginary conversations with the members of his master mind group. Twenty-six years after reading William Nickerson's book, we had dinner with him and were able to thank him personally for his inspiration and guidance.

Invest In Yourself

Every time you read a book or attend a workshop or class, you are investing in yourself. Benjamin Franklin said "Empty the coins from your purse into your mind and your mind will fill your purse to overflowing."

When we first started our investment pro-gram, we drove to Chicago once a week for two years to study property management in classes sponsored by the Institute of Real Estate Manage-ment. Whatever skill you want to acquire or area of expertise you want to develop, find out who are the authorities in that field. Read their books, and whenever possible, study with them personally.

We have always put a high value on education and consider the money well spent when we get one good new idea from a book or class. Over the years we have attended dozens of seminars.

In 1982 I took a workshop called "The Radiance Technique (sm): The Official Reiki Program®" with Dr. Barbara Ray, author of "The Reiki Factor." Reiki is the Science of Universal Energy, and the technique offered a method for managing stress, promoting positive wellness, expanding creativity and supporting personal growth.

I was so impressed with the results from the applications of this technique that I continued to study and work with it and in 1986 became a teacher of The Radiance Technique(sm). (For a list of teachers in the U.S. and abroad, write the American-International Reiki Association, Inc., 2210 Wilshire Blvd., Suite 831, Santa Monica, CA. 90403.)

10 Steps to a Million Dollars

When we first decided to become millionaires, I had a problem. The goal was too far-fetched for me to imagine it. After all, the first year we were married our combined earnings were less than $5,000.

I solved my problem by looking at it in a new way. I learned that if you start with $1,000 and double it ten times, you'll end up with more than a million dollars. Sounds crazy, doesn't it, but try it yourself. Count the steps off on your fingers: 1) $2,000 2) $4,000 . . .all the way to 10). $1,024,000.

I also learned the principle of doubling our money, and each step became for me 10% of the journey to a million dollars. How long will it take to double your money? The Rule of 72 will tell you. Divide the interest rate your investment is earning into 72, and the result is the number of years it will take for your money to double. For example, at 12% interest, you will double your money in six years; at 24% interest you will double it in 3 years.

On the chart that I drew up, $32,000 was the fifth step, or 50% of the road to a million dollars. Anyone who develops the discipline necessary to save the initial $1,000, invest it wisely and proceed to double her money five times has laid the foundation for the next five steps. Actually, it's much harder to turn $2,000 into $4,000 than it is to turn $200,000 into $400,000.

Women have the potential to be terrific investors since they are such good shoppers. Instead of investing so much time and effort into buying $100 worth of groceries for $75, why not put the same effort into buying a $10,000 investment for $7,500, or even better, a $100,000 investment for $75,000? Many women have become wealthy by applying their shopping expertise to buying undervalued single family homes.

Along the Way Take Time to Smell the Flowers

While camping at Peninsula State Park in Door County, Wisconsin, many years ago, a plaque in a souvenir shop caught my attention. Its message was: "Along the way take time to smell the flowers." We brought the plaque home and hung it in our living room. It has become our family motto.

Be the Creator of Your Life

You can go through life reacting to the demands of other people and circumstances and letting them control your life, or you can choose to create your own life, one choice at a time. In the long run, it's more satisfying to accept the responsibility for all aspects of your life, including your financial destiny.

Write to me and I'll send you a gift— some million dollar bills that you can use to keep yourself motivated and *expand your prosperity consciousness.*

Dr. C. R. BAILEY
Magnatron Sales Co., Inc.
1301 Meadow Sweet Road
Golden, CO 80401
(303)477-4857 (303)238-I534

Dr. C. R. Bailey

Dr. "C. R." Bailey, who lives with his wife Ruby in Denver, Colorado, is Vice-President of Marketing for Magnatron Sales Company. His responsibilities include networking with manufacturers of the major brands of computer supplies and marketing those products to major corporations.

Dr. Bailey is an author and popular speaker. He is featured on TV shows, and in many newspaper and magazine articles. He is featured in numerous "Who's Who" publications, has served in the U.S. Navy, and in Church Administration.

Dr. Bailey represented Gov. Lamm and Mayor Mc Nichols, directing work with several Korean cities. These working relations still continue.

Motivated Managers

By Dr. C. R. Bailey

"No man is an Island, entire of itself.
Any man's death diminishes me,
because I am involved in Mankind:
And therefore never send to know
for whom the bell tolls:
It tolls for thee."   — John Donne

Over twenty years ago, a suburb of Chicago was faced with a critical water shortage. The community voted a bond issue and built a dam to solve the problem. But they suffered for seven more years from the same miserable situation. Then a water department worker discovered that three main valves at the city's reservoir were only partially opened. They did not need a dam, or a bond issue, they needed to open the floodgates. The flow had never diminished.

The principles written and applied within this chapter will help you find your main valves and release them. Now is the time to stop creative rationing. Motivated managers can assist their co-workers to locate their restrictions and OPEN THEM UP.

There Is a Negative Side

Just as Japanese horticulturists have made a fine art of raising dwarf trees, there are some managers in responsible positions who make a fine art of raising "dwarf workers."

The miniature tree and the full-sized tree start out the same size. At the first sign of root growth, the miniature tree's roots are cut and trimmed immediately. The full-sized tree's roots are allowed to grow. One becomes a giant, one is dwarfed.

Too many allow others to cut and trim their creative roots at first sign of growth. You must be prepared to object to any outside force chipping and cutting away at your mental roots. You have the power and the right to make decisions which will enhance your growth.

There is more. You have the power and the right to overcome the negative root killers which have dwarfed and stifled your growth in the past.

Broom At The Top?

The trouble with American business today is in the corporate offices, not on the assembly line, stated H. Ross Perot to a group of judges, lawyers and public officals recently. Perot criticized management decisions and said new attitudes and business strategies must be developed to deal with foreign competitors. He disputed claims that workers in the United States are less productive than workers in Japan.

The big challenge of the 1980's is not the retraining of the workers, it is the retraining of the managers, according to John Naisbitt, author of "Reinventing the Corporation."

Management Is Motivating Other People

The only way you can motivate people is to communicate with them. You've got to know how to talk with them. The key to Motivated Management is plain and simple.

Movitated Managers know the key to success is not information. It is people. They fill the top management spots with eager beavers. These are the ones who do more than they are expected to. Motivated Managers know how to delegate, to motivate others. They find the pressure points, and set priorities. They know what can be done now. They do not wait for "pie in the sky" to develop. They are movers, shakers, and change makers.

Motivated Managers
Use These Basic Questions:

1. What are your objectives for the next quar ter?
2. Will you show me your plans for this month? Today?
3. What are your priorities?
4. What are the obstacles you must overcome to achieve these objectives?
5. Will you show me your overall game plan?

Good management and motivation help people set their own goals. They allow the worker to become productive, and self-motivated. They help new ideas surface which give fresh approaches to problem-solving, and keep people from getting lost within the system.

Fine management forces good communication. A top manager gathers all available information, sets a time allotment, calls the team together, then acts.

We Are All in the Process of Building

Our personal buildings display much about ourselves. While some build dream castles — others stack high prison walls around their lives.

It takes no longer to build a castle than it does a prison. Either takes preparation. Don't be misled when told that everyone has twenty-four hours each day, seven days each week. UNTRUE!

We only have the hours per day in which we act upon our own goals and plans. These are the construction days that count for our future. Thomas Carlyle said, "Be careful what you think about, for you will surely get it." Be careful what life you build for yourself, for you must live in it. YOU are the architect of the structure, good or bad.

Don't Wait For Others to Bring Your Dreams to Fruition

Can you imagine interviewing Greg LeMond, the only American to win the Tour de France bicycle race, immediately after the event? You ask him, "Would you tell me the preparation you went through for this race?"

Would he answer, "Well, it was a nice day, and I was out riding my bike. I saw this large group of bikers. I just decided to join them on the spur of the moment."

Of course this is not what happened, nor would he ever say this. He trained many long and enduring months of preparation for this race. He paid the price. Preparation. It is not the high price of success people object to, it is the ruinous price of failure that hurts.

Self Esteem

A few years ago, my wife Ruby and I went to vote in an election. We arrived, got the ballots and started to our separate voting booths. Ruby said "C.R., did you know your name is on the ballot?"

My response was, "What are you talking about?" I was shocked. When they had asked me to serve, I had no idea there would be a vote on the matter. It gave me a great deal of satisfaction to vote for myself that day.

As we go to work each day, we all need to vote for ourselves. Self-esteem and self acceptance are motivation for ourselves. Then we can motivate others.

Fear of Failure

Fear of failure is the enemy of self-esteem, a psychosis which literally causes many to reject personal exploration. It is costly to our personal and professional growth. It is the father of tunnel vision, and is fatal to personal experimentation. Fear of failure stacks up the bricks of our self-constructed prison.

One of the great tragedies of our modern society is the fear of making a mistake. Conformists and pseudointellectuals believe that "mistake" is something to be ashamed of. To be ashamed of making a mistake is the greatest error of all.

While living in San Jose, Costa Rica, I studied the Spanish language. My frustration in trying to communicate with someone in their own language, having such a limited vocabulary myself, was frightening. There is only one way to increase vocabulary and improve enunciation. Make mistakes.

I learned to laugh at myself, and learn from my stumbling errors. There is nothing wrong in making a mistake through lack of knowledge, experience or considered judgement. We only grow by falling and getting up, like a little child learning to walk.

We Are the Construction Crew

Mental obsessions manifest themselves in a physical manner. Our most dreaded fears have a way of happening. We re-enact the happening. If we leave our driving license at home, we remember we don't have it with us.

Just then we approach a patrol car from the rear. We think, "I hope he does not stop me, I left my license at home."

Then our driving becomes erratic through fear. The officer pulls us over. Our thought brought about the feared action. We built our own prison wall.

Change Fear From Negative to Positive

FEAR SAYS: " Do I have to? I wish I could... IF ONLY... Why should I be the one to do it? Look at all the problems... Well, I'll try... I just can't MAKE it... I will go on to the next job."

FAITH SAYS: "It is a pleasure to do it. I am excited about it. I can SEE the opportunity. Look at the potential. This challenge demands a winning team effort. I can visualize the job done now. I am excited about the possibilities of my work."

Motivating Others

Motivation is defined as :
1. Influence of current behavior.
2. Cause of action. Providing a motive.
3. Control of the inner drive of a person.
4. That force which causes motion within a person.
5. An inner quality that demands outward manifestation.
6. An idea or desire expected to be realized.

Types of Motivation

1. FEAR: This is the easiest type. However, fear is also many times the least effective type of motivation, if used over a long period of time. It will work for a while, but can you imagine a 30 year old son constantly being fearful of a 55 year old father?

2.   INCENTIVE: Incentive motivation promises rewards for reaching goals. It is the famous stick with a dangling carrot. Incentive motivation promises rewards for reaching another person's goal.

3.   ATTITUDE: Attitude forces us to look within ourselves and come up with answers. Some people will not accept responsibility because it might provide an opportunity for growth. When we change our attitude toward our family, friends, work, and most importantly toward ourselves, we alter the basic structure of our own personality.

Attitude motivation is not a quick fix for an old problem. It is much like taking boiling water from the stove and placing an ice cube in it. What happens? First, the ice melts. Second, the temperature of the boiling water decreases.

One small ice cube will not make boiling water refreshing to a thirsty person. But if you keep up the process, the water will become cool and thirst quenching. The heat represents negative attitudes. The cool refreshing water is the positive attitude. It takes time. The water did not start boiling in an instant. It will not cool down in an instant either.

We are where we are, and what we are now, because of what we have allowed to go into our minds. We can change what we are by altering the input. We have the freedom to do so. We are the builders of our lives.

Spaced Repetition

Mary had a little...
Its fleece was white as...

It may have been 10, 20 or even 40 years since you first heard this poem, but you probably can go on to the next two lines, and maybe even complete the 2nd verse. Why? because you have heard it over and over, you remember every word of it. Reading, listening to tapes, watching views in your field, constantly learning and re-learning, instills confidence.

Sir Isaac Newton said, "I stood on the shores of time and occasionally picked up a beautiful shell or two. But all in front of me stretched out the great sea — all undiscovered."

Never Stop Learning

Fear of failure is overcome with the self-confidence of knowlege, and of practical experience. Experience is knowledge in action. It is achieved after confrontation and engagement. Fear of failure comes from lack of experience and basic information.

The employee or manager with fear of failure is always waiting. It is never the right time or circumstance. The longer the wait, the greater the fear.

Invisible Barriers

On Miami Beach, Florida, where my family lived, there was a savage barracuda swimming in the same tank of water with a spanish mackerel. Normally the barracuda would attack and eat the mackerel. But not so here.

For several weeks there was a clear transparent barrier placed between the two fish. The barracuda would go for the mackerel and hit the barrier. The mackerel would flee to the far end of the water tank. After several bruising crashes into the transparent barrier, the barracuda was content to swim in a small circle in his end of the tank.

Now the barrier was removed. Guess what happened. Nothing! The barracuda still swam in his end of the tank, the mackerel circled nonchalantly at the other end with no fear whatsoever. The only barrier was in their minds.

When our own self-imposed barriers of limitations are removed, are we still waiting and waiting? Too many stories are yet to be written. Too many dreams have died a-borning. How many go to their graves with their songs unsung? They are stopped up. Not by circumstance, but by the block of inertia. Inertia is lack of imagination.

Rodin's statue, the "Thinker" is symbolized mankind asking "What if?" Can we imagine going over, under, around, using new combinations? Strong will does not remove barriers. Only positive imagination offers alternatives. With imagination, the bastions of defeat are stormed. Every job attempted removes barriers and provides experience and confidence for the next opportunity.

Motivated Managers learn success is *not* a destination. It is a journey. Winning is not everything. But our winning effort *is*. Do not be afraid to make a new effort every day of your life.

Change Your Thinking

- From "Why pay the price?" to: "Enjoy the benefits and opportunities."
- From "Fear of failure," to: "Dare to dream of a new way."
- From "What will others think?" to: "They all want me to win!"

Very few of us would be concerned about what others thought of us if we really knew how seldom they did. It is what we think of ourselves that comes first. "First to your ownself be true," as Shakespeare explains, and then it must follow as night follows day, we cannot be false to anyone.

Some years ago, Ruby, Kathy, and James surprised me with a Scottie terrier puppy for Christmas. I named her Lass. She took a place in our hearts and home right away. In a few months when warmer weather was upon us, Lass was overdue for a haircut.

When our family arrived home after her trip to the dog groomer, we were amazed. Lass looked so different than we had ever seen her before. The children laughed. Lass ducked her head and hid under the table.

For over a week, each time we entered the room, Lass ducked her head and crawled away under the nearest furniture. The next time we took her to the dog groomer, we gave strict instructions that no one was to laugh at her when she returned home. We all were to make over her, pet her, and tell her how beautiful she looked. Our plan was carried out.

Lass strutted! She knew she was beautiful, and acted enthusiastically because we told her she was wonderful. The difference was in her mind.

How many poor managers have discouraged good ideas by derisive laughter, or snide remarks? Will Shakespeare said, "The sun will not be up as soon as I, to greet the fair adventure of tomorrow!" Motivatived managers have great expectations for all those they manage.

Even more seriously, how many of us have been so frightened of cruel laughter that we let our own fear stop us from the great adventure of life?

How Motivated Managers Work

"Love your neighbor as you love yourself." How fortunate I was to have a mother who taught me the principals of Jesus.

Movitated managers encourage others. They praise often; criticize very little, and then only after praising.

SELF	OTHERS
1. Learn self-respect.	Show respect for others.
2. Forgive yourself.	Forgive others.
3. Do not take yourself too seriously.	Do not take the needs of others lightly.
4. Take your work seriously.	Respect the work of others.
5. Laugh at yourself.	Do not laugh at others.
6. Be your own best friend.	Be a true friend to others.

What Do Motivated Managers Give?

What are the positive aspects which you might expect from Motivated Managers? Here is my list. It is only the beginning of ways I have been helped. <u>Motivated Managers</u>:

- Care about me, and how I am progressing.
- Help me refine my thoughts before I blurt them out.
- Challenge me to do my best.
- Allow me to make decisions (good and bad).
- Assist me to understand rules and regulations.
- Keep a confidence.
- Help me keep my objectivity.
- Set a good example, and inspire me to follow.
- Are a source of encouragement.

- Give me recognition when I deserve it.
- Celebrate with me when our goals are accomplished.

Point of View

Some managers dismissed the huge Mary Kay cosmetic annual seminar held in Dallas, Texas, as "mere theatrics," or "show business." But Tom Peters tells us all business is show business. The very symbol of values and benefits.

Dr. Norman Vincent Peale enjoys telling the story about the man who was such a grump in church that it was noticeable to those about him.

One Sunday, as "Jeff" was leaving he complained, "I don't understand why everyone is putting on such a show."

"What do you mean?" replied Dr. Peale.

"All this laughing and putting on a false front here at church," Jeff growled.

Dr. Peale said," I know what will make you the same way, Jeff. You can be happy too. But I am not going to tell you how to be happy, because you will not do what I suggest."

"I will do anything you suggest if it will honestly make me happy," Jeff promised.

So Dr. Peale told him what to do. "Every night before you go to bed, pray for your competitors. Ask God to give them more business the next day than He gives you."

"You tricked me!" Jeff screamed. "You tricked

me!" Dr. Peale smiled. "I told you that you would not do it."

"Well, I WILL DO IT!" Jeff yelled defiantly, and walked away.

The following Sunday Dr. Peale could see no noticeable difference except that perhaps Jeff was a litttle worse than ever. Two more Sundays went by.

Dr. Peale thought he saw a hint of a smile on Jeff's face during church. Following the service, Dr. Peale asked how Jeff was doing.

"The first few nights as I asked God to help my competitors get more business than He would give me, well, I would pray, then I got in bed and asked God to forgive me for lying! After a while though, I meant my prayer. A few more days went by and I met one of my competitors. Actually I found he is a nice guy. This week I plan to have lunch with a couple more of my competitors." **And Jeff smiled.**

People are Important

Wherever motivated managers find them, people are important. They deserve positive attention and good will. When motivated managers evaluate the value of a worker they remember the old adage: "The value is in the doer, not the deed."

The operating of a business boils down to people, product and profit. Motivated managers never forget, people come *first*. When a good team works together, the odds for success are greatly improved. Without good people first, the product and profit fail.

Lee Iacocca: Movitated Manager

Lee Iacocca tells about the people he required to help him turn Chrysler Corporation around. They did not help because of Lee's salesmanship. He called out the kind of people who responded to challenge. They stuck with him even when it wasn't any fun. They had inner strength. "It was an adventure," Lee explained.

Movitated managers have one very important common factor in their lives. They have the ability to see the strengths in other people and to call them out.

'Turn It Loose!'

One rainy morning at Whiting Field, a Navy Air Station outside Pensacola Florida, a maintenance test pilot stopped beside one of the twelve planes in my group. He asked me to take a test hop with him.

After checking out a parachute I joined him. As we took off he explained that the plane had an engine change. This was the first flight for that new engine. We climbed to 10,000 feet. We went over the parachuting procedures. He asked me to take off my shoulder harness, but keep my parachute buckled, then to relax.

Then we went into a spiral and a loop. I fell all over myself, and could not keep from hitting the instrument panel. I hit head first on the canopy, then from side to side. I grabbed the canopy release to parachute to safety.

Over the head set he screamed, "Turn it loose! Turn it loose!"

We leveled off, and set the plane down. The pilot asked me if I had planned to leave him stranded with a crippled aircraft at 10,000 feet. My reply was, "I sure couldn't help you. You bet, I was leaving."

He cursed me for attempting to leave him alone. Then he asked me this question: "Are you sure you did the right thing?"

I assured him that I did. He rubbed his hand over my headset and said: "You're my man. You did exactly the right thing. You acted properly under pressure. I want you to fly with me on my test hops." He encouraged me and instilled confidence. Two years later, he crashed and died serving our wonderful country.

Motivated managers see good in other people. They also have the ability to see good in difficult situations. What they project to others is projected back to them. Life is much like a mirror.

Good Business

Movitated Managers let workers know what is going on in the company.

The more the workers DON'T know, the more they guess wrong about the status of the future of their company.

One "C.E.O." asked his managers to write down what they thought company profits were for the past year. He was shocked to see how much the managers over-estimated. Another misconception by managers was where the profits were going. They were amazed as they learned how much it cost just to keep up with the expansion program.

A program of openness is now over fifteen years old in this particular company. One of the managers was asked what he liked most about his work. He answered, "If I had to tell you in one sentence why I am motivated on my job, it is because I know what is going on, and how I fit into the overall picture. That makes me feel important."

Motivated Managers bring every employee into the overall picture. They make customers, employees, everyone "feel important."

Great people are meteors designed to burn so that the earth may be lighted.   - Napoleon

MICHAEL J. CRANDAL
Performance Enhancement Specialists
86 Sandhurst Road
Mundelein, IL 60060
(312)362-4724

Michael J. Crandal

In addition to the "just give me the facts" information, Michael J. Crandal is noted for offering liberal doses of personal insight, humor, and warmth. He has succeeded in balancing a childhood from the mountains of Idaho, to "scaling the mountains" of today's competitive business world.

During the past 10+ years he has worked closely with many corporate boards of directors and has rubbed elbows with numerous top executives and business people throughout the United States. In each instance, his goal has been to have them all not only emerge as a better businessperson... but a better person as well.

His speeches and seminars on the development of leadership skills and Performance Enhancement have been enthusiastically received by top-level executives, managers and professional educators.

He is a past member of the board of directors for the HOPE school for the Blind. Presently, he is a member of the American Association of Professional Cunsultants, Midwest Society of Professional Consultants, National Federation of Independent Business, Center for Entrepreneurial Management, National Business Education Association, National Management Association, International Platform Association, and the Club Managers Association of America.

He is author of The Power Tools of Performance Enhancement *and has articles published in numerous magazines.*

You've Got to Make a Little Dust in This World

By Michael J. Crandal

*" If you refuse to play the game -
You automatically lose the game."*

People do not buy quality. Strange as that may seem, it is a truth. People do not buy quality... what they do buy, however, is <u>perceived</u> quality, and this is the reason why high-powered, major, multi-billion dollar corporations are presenting slick designed and produced media blitz campaigns that do everything to promote glamour, romance, prestige and sex appeal... yet do nothing to inform you about their product itself.

Why do they do this? Obviously they have learned through market research and analysis that the consumer buys image and perceived quality rather than a product. For this reason:

AUTO MANUFACTURERS actively market sex-appeal and prestige... much more so than a mode of transportation.

TOBACCO COMPANIES actively market macho image and adventure...rather than the joys of inhaling hot smoke.

BREWERIES actively market having friends and socializing... more so than drinking beer.

An enormous portion of the American business dollar is invested in the advertising and marketing fields. In some quarters, it is a fact that corporate allowance of monies for the purpose of marketing their products far exceeds the total amount expended on research development and production of the products themselves.

Hundreds of millions of dollars are spent to decide critical issues such as the following:

ON THE DRY CEREAL PACKAGE IN GROCERY
STORES... Should the baseball hero be
shown swinging a bat or would it better
enhance sales if he were instead shown
sliding head first into second base?

IN MAGAZINE PAGES ON OUR COFFEE
TABLES...
Should the young modern couple (with love
in their eyes and cigarettes in their hands)

be shown outside the chauffeur driven
limousine looking like they are just
leaving for an exciting night on the town...
or would it better enhance sales if instead
it looked as if they were just returning from
that same exciting night?

ON THE BILLBOARDS ALONG OUR HIGHWAYS...
Should a nice looking girl be shown right in
the middle of what appears to be a surprise
party in her honor surrounded by her clos-
est friends all with beer in their hands... or
would it better enhance sales to show a
man alone next to a mountain campfire at
dusk with a can of beer?

OVER THE RADIOS IN OUR CARS...
Should the listener be subjected to jet tur-
bine engines roaring off and fading into the
imagined sunset while a soothing voice
suggests that it could be you in one of those
first-class seats taking off to exotic places...
or would it better enhance ticket sales to
have gentle tropical music in the background as that same voice tells you about
the frequency of departure times?

ON THE TELEVISION IN OUR FAMILY ROOMS...
Should the local, small town independent
gas station owner be shown efficiently attending to the needs of his customers... or
would sales be better enhanced by a brief
documentary highlighting the process of oil
exploration under the ocean floor with only
the company logo shown in silence at

the end?

The point of all this is <u>not</u> to encourage you to seek a new career in the advertising and marketing fields. The point <u>is</u> to encourage you to immediately come to grips with the reality that your personal success can be greatly influenced by the advertising and marketing strategies you apply to yourself.

Selling YOU

Diversified corporations may have a multitude of products and have spent millions of dollars establishing a plan to market them. Contrary to a corporation, you as an "independent operator," are your only product line. YOU are the only product you have to sell. If we assume for just a moment that the money giant corporations spend on marketing their products is money well spent... then doesn't it also make sense that we too, as individuals, should spend some time and effort in marketing ourselves? It only follows that you should spend the time needed establishing a plan to market your only product... **YOU!**

However... again, contrary to many major corporate powers we have the pleasure of hearing from every day... let us not lose sight of the fact that there is indeed no substitute for quality. Simple, yet it deserves repeating: THERE IS NO SUBSTITUTE FOR QUALITY!

We must never forget that there is a tremendous difference between merely looking good and really *being* good. The individual (or company for that matter) who stresses only one or the other is potentially headed for short term gains with long term losses.

A successful individual (company) knows that while looking good is a vital marketing tool... that alone is not enough to perpetuate long-range permanent returns on investment. Behind all of the glossy Fifth Avenue corporate logo design and that slick show-biz corporate slogan... there <u>must</u> be a product of quality design, quality concept and quality workmanship!

On the other hand— once a quality finished product is ready for distribution, in order to initiate any "first time" sales, there quite obviously must be some structured marketing plan letting the consumer know the availability of the product.

Repeat sales are the name of the game. You can't get repeat sales if when all is said and done — you really have nothing to sell. It must be understood that repeat sales and word of mouth advertising are the name of the game.

Advertising can be equated to the icing on a beautifully decorated cake. For no matter how beautiful the cake may look from the outside and no matter how wonderful it appears... we are not going to take a second chance if we find that once we cut through the icing we find that there is no cake— only a cardboard facsimile.

In terms of positioning yourself for success — you are no different in many ways to the corporate giants. You, too, must develop yourself into a quality product and then follow through with a well-thought-out marketing plan geared towards letting the "consumer" know of your availability and the quality of your product... that being *you.*

Get the Customer's Attention

In order to be in a position to sell anything — from your company, your corporate image, your services, or most importantly yourself— you <u>must</u> draw attention. Once you have their attention you are then (and only then) in a position to make an initial sale. After that first sale then the quality of your product should kick in just like the afterburners of a rocket and become a primary factor in creating repeat sales.

My personal experience taught me the value of getting the customer's attention. My adventures as a waiter when I was a young man encouraged me to better and better my presentation skills for two reasons: 1) I had a white-hot desire to do my very best and to enjoy the inner satisfaction of doing so, and 2) The harder I worked at polishing my skills, the better my gratuities became.

As I strove hard to improve my skills, there was an immediate, one-to-one ratio between my performance vs. my tips. The harder I worked toward my goal to be a truly professional and polished waiter — the better and better the monetary returns of my efforts became. But then something very perplexing happened. Just when

I began to really feel that my people skills were sharpened to a finely honed degree, I began to experience a slight decrease in my tips. Try as I wanted to believe that this must be just "one of those things" and that things would iron themselves out as the weeks wore on, ironically, I found that as the weeks drifted away, so did the returns on my tables.

I responded to this fact by working even harder to further add polish to my existing skills and to learn new ones at the same time. I was sure that soon the gratuities would not only return to their old lofty heights, but would also surpass them. Such was not the case. What happened was that I had reached that point known as the "Law of Diminishing Returns."

While there seemed to be a direct ratio between effort and return in the early stages of my development... this failed to be true despite my continuing efforts toward becoming more professional and polished. The answer became clear to me as I analyzed the problem. The symptom was that my tips were going down — the problem was that I no longer had the customer's attention!

My earlier efforts were, at times, the center of attention since it was often necessary for me to interrupt the guests to clarify something I did not understand or to make extra trips to the table when I had overlooked something. Now, don't get me wrong... I do not wish to present an image of a totally inept waiter with a lack of training... I do, however, wish to paint a picture of a young man at your table who, even though a bit wet behind the ears, was able to provide a very enjoyable evening; a young man who was clearly working very hard to do his best, and quite frankly, was doing a pretty good job of it at that. Should a mild mishap occur, I would handle it with such people-pleasing grace and warmth that I perhaps came out looking better than if the mishap had never happened at all. *And that was the point!!! That was the problem later on!!!*

When small mishaps, no matter what their nature, would occur — I would handle them strictly as an opportunity to look good. And after doing so... more times than not, upon returning to the table, I would be the center of a conversation about what a good waiter I was. But as I became better and better at the mechanics of being a waiter, I had less and less opportunity to use my people skills simply because there were no longer any mishaps to smooth over. I had become invisible. I had become a very effective waiter— but an equally ineffective source of income.

Keep the Customer's Attention

Sooooooo... after having analyzed the problem, I set out to solve it. I had to regain the attention of the customer. I began by *intentionally* creating a small mishap and then handling. it. The following was my favorite ploy: When serving coffee after dinner, I would intentionally not bring the cream to a particular guest whom I knew preferred it. I would, however, bring the cream with me and set it out of sight, a few steps away from the table. After having poured the coffee, I would suddenly, yet in a gentlemanly manner, interrupt the table and offer them a most sincere apology for neglecting to bring the gentleman his cream. I would assure them that I would, of course, remedy this bit of negligence on my part immediately!

When I returned to the table, I was once again hearing conversations about what a simply marvelous waiter I was. Just as I had initially projected, my gratuities not only returned to their old stature, but surpassed them several times over.

Let me add one bit of further insight to the above story. It must be clearly understood that had I waited too long to mention the lack of cream — and it was the customer who had to mention it to me — it would have been too late. At that point my efforts could have backfired.

So, the message is this: YOU HAVE TO GET THEIR ATTENTION... AND AFTER DOING SO, YOU HAVE GOT TO BE IN CONTROL OF THE SITUATION TO BEST POSITION YOURSELF FOR SUCCESS!

You will often come in contact with people who talk big about who they are and all of the wonderful things they can do for you. This behavior is contrary to the confident achiever who moves steadily and speaks in quiet tones. Never fall prey to the phony idea that the best method to promote yourself is by "tooting your own horn" and making unfounded promises about the quality of your work. Never forget that you will always open more doors by asking intelligent questions than you will by offering lame answers.

If you refuse to play the game... you automatically lose the game. Those individuals who appreciate the fact that they must not only look good, but also *be* good, are the same ones who will soon be courting success in this big beautiful world. Those who refuse to play the game by rationalizing, "Phooey! I'm not going to play games with anyone by working on some silly old image. I know who I am and what I can do, and that is enough for me. I don't have to play games or prove anything to anybody but myself!" These are the same people who never really understand why others around them with equal or only slightly better skills seem to rocket past them towards greater success. (That is when you hear them muttering to themselves, "Aw, they just got lucky!")

Sadly, quality alone is not enough. And, fortunately, marketing and advertising alone are not enough. Long range success must combine the two ingredients... with the heavy emphasis on quality.

Successful people are not those who have no problems, but rather, people who handle problems well. Handling problems is where the real performer rises to the top. A true quality performer is one who has the insight to recognize potential problem areas in their early stages of development... and then takes the appropriate action to solve problems BEFORE they happen!

Any problem that comes up is really only an opportunity for an achiever to achieve.

The Value of Hard Work

In developing your own marketing strategies for yourself, start with the basics:

- Take pride in your personal grooming h a b - its. Always do your best to look your best.
- Practice speaking in clear and precise terms.
- Make a habit of standing erect, yet relaxed.
- Walk like you have a destination in mind.
- Be direct and open in dealing with others.
- Never forget the value of the opinions and feelings of others.
- Be a "doer" — don't just talk a good game.
- Whenever possible, compliment those around you.
- Never forget that honesty is, indeed, the best policy.
- Above all — when all "marketing" is said and done, don't ever forget the value of hard work.

Several times during the course of this chapter you will note that some points are repeated again and again to emphasize the importance of key concepts that you will want to have locked in your mind. With that thought... I want to repeat one thing from the list above that cannot be said too often... DO NOT EVER FORGET THE VALUE OF HARD WORK!

Let me share with you a few personal experiences that vividly illustrate this all-important concept.

My first management job was with a major hotel chain based in Minneapolis, Minnesota. The property where I was employed was located in Lincoln, Nebraska. My position was that of restaurant manager and my responsibilities included the supervision of three different and distinct food and beverage outlets in a nine story hotel. Approximately 60 employees were included in my jurisdiction and I reported directly to the food and beverage director of the hotel and indirectly to the property general manager. (Not bad for a young man of 19 years!) My normal work day was from 5 p.m. to approximately 1 a.m. I mention the number of employees I was responsible for and the size of the hotel only to emphasize that there was really a lot of work to do... especially for a young man striving to do his best to excel. There were times when I knew that I was in over my head and that only through determination and hard work was I going to succeed and achieve the results I desired. Believe me, I had my hands full! And even though I was doing quite well and working very hard at it — I knew that this was not enough. I sensed that if I were to develop only my restaurant management skills, but do nothing more, rather than becoming one of the best restaurant managers at an early age, as the years passed, I would become and remain an adequate restaurant manager at an older age. I knew that I had to do more; I knew that I had to draw attention to myself.

In order to get that attention, and to expose myself to the opportunity of learning new and different skills at the same time, I made a point of coming to work at 2 or 3 in the afternoon rather than the expected 5 o'clock. I also made a point of staying around the hotel until 2 or 3 in the morning. My point is not to advocate becoming a "workaholic," but simply to suggest that hard work will not kill you and can be one of your greatest calling cards, separating you from the great many also-rans. I spent those extra hours on the job for one specific reason. During my 5 to 1 shift, my time was completely taken up by those duties which directly related to my position. I was, therefore, limiting my ability to learn and grow. By simply being at the hotel and "marketing" my availability and the quality of my work, I was able to help out in other departments and be exposed to new skills.

I was soon gathering tidbits about how to operate the front desk of a hotel... I learned about the operation of a centralized storeroom... I was exposed to a great deal of useful, and marketable, skills that I would never have had the opportunity to learn had I been content to do only the job asked of me. Things would come up at the hotel and fall my direction. The word was: "Well, why don't you ask Michael to do that? After all, he is available and willing to help!"

Obviously, in order to be marketable, you

must have some set of skills or services that are ready for the market place. The very best way to learn new skills and to develop services is through hard work. After skills and services have been accumulated to a high degree, you will find that the actual hours spent working may decline. This is not to suggest that contentment and lack of motivation have set in. Far from it. It is simply an indication that, as a result of hard work, you have positioned yourself to start working smarter — not necessarily harder.

Hard Work and 'Luck'

There are, of course, those individuals who scoff at others for working too hard since they themselves feel it necessary to do only enough to get by without drawing any attention to themselves. They mock those who begin to move ahead by making trivial rationalizations like, "Pooh-pooh... They were just lucky." Remember, and remember it well — THE HARDER YOU WORK THE LUCKIER YOU GET!

A few years later I had a similar experience as my career path began to take shape. I happened to notice in the want ads that there was a need for an experienced person to prepare the weekly payroll and quarterly tax reports for the business where I was employed. I was only one of about 120 employees and knew nothing about payroll preparation or tax reports. I also knew that if I did not concern myself with anything other than accomplishing the work I was directly responsible for... I never would learn these skills.

So, I contacted the general manager of the facility and told him that I had seen the ad in the classified section of the newspaper. He seemed pleased and asked if I knew of someone I could recommend to fill the position. I told him as a matter of fact I did... ME! I openly admitted that I had no skills that qualified me for the job other than my desire to learn and my willingness to work hard. I further explained that I would be happy to do the job with no increase in my present salary and that in no way would I allow this added responsibility to affect the performance of my other duties. I made it very clear that I would consider the opportunity to learn as my compensation for doing the work. The only real "cost" would be that my proposition would require the company to invest the time to teach me the needed skills to do the job. It was a "WIN-WIN" situation. The company wins in that they have filled a need to have the payroll and taxes done. I win due to the fact that I created the opportunity to develop new skills— very marketable skills!

I soon found myself preparing the weekly payroll and quarterly tax reports! LET'S PUT **WORK** IN OUR VOCABULARY!!!

I'd like to share with you an excerpt from a quote by Bob Burdette that is included in a collection called <u>Elbert Hubbard's Scrap Book</u>:
"... Remember you have to work. Whether you handle pick or wheelbarrow or a set of books, digging ditches or editing a newspaper,   ring-

ing an auction bell or writing funny things, you must work. Don't be afraid of killing yourself... men die sometimes, but it is because they quit work at 9:00 p.m. and don't go home until 2:00 a.m. It's the intervals that kill... Work gives you appetite for your meals; it lends solidity to your slumber and gives you perfect appreciation for a holiday... So, find out what you want to be and do, take off your coat and **make dust in the world.** The busier you are, the less harm you are apt to get into, the sweeter will be your sleep, the brighter your holidays, and the better satisfied the whole world will be with you."

'In a race, everyone runs, but only one person gets first prize. So run your race to win.'

1 Corinthians 9:24

Successful people in this world are those who get up and look for the circumstances they want. If they can't find them, they make them.

— George Bernard Shaw

DAWAR A. SHAH
P. O. Box 4690
West Covina, CA 91791
(818)919-0690 (818)962-2408

Dawar A. Shah

Dawar A. Shah was born in Pakistan, a country in South Asia on the Arabian Sea. He joined the Pakistan Air Force in 1970, where he graduated as a pilot officer with a Bachelor of Science Degree. Dawar served as a squadron fighter pilot and instructor pilot before voluntarily resigning from the Air Force.

After leaving the Air Force, he served various organizations as a charter instructor/pilot. After declining a job offer as a pilot for an International Airline, Dawar embarked on the "Aircraft of Entrepreneurism."

Dawar Shah is a great innovator. He has developed a unique way of acquiring advanced education. He has traveled the world meeting extremely successful entrepreneurs. They have revealed the secrets of their successes to him. Dawar has carefully made notes of their experiences.

In January, 1982 he migrated to the United States. He is owner and president of a successful import/export company which imports oriental rugs from overseas. He is a writer, speaker, and sought after marketing consultant. He consults in the areas of direct mail, advertising, mail order and foreign trade. Dawar (rhymes with power) Shah has a business success philosophy he preaches everywhere: "Being a Millionaire may never satisfy you, but helping a fraction of a million people **will certainly do so.**"

How to Achieve
the "Winner's Edge"
in Your Business Life

By Dawar Shah

"A Friend is the one who comes in the door,
-When the whole world just went out."
                    - Dottie Walters

Before I share with you four powerful ways to
achieve that all important "winners edge" for your
business, I would like to tell you a true story of my
life when I was a flight instructor in the Air Force
Academy of my native country, Pakistan.

This dramatic incident changed the way I look at life's challenges. I am sure you will find this story interesting, and hope it may serve as food for thought for you when you meet a difficult situation. It holds great significance for me.

It was a bright sunny morning in May, 1977. I was flying with one of the student pilots (we will call him Tom), giving him practice in take-offs and landings. We were flying a T-37 twin engine American built Jet trainer. This aircraft is used by many countries of the the world, to train Military pilots.

Tom had already acquired some flying experience and had recently done his first "solo" flight. Solo flight implies that a student is cleared to fly A/C all by himself, after he has shown enough competence in handling of the aircraft without any assistance from an instructor pilot. The student must especially show proficiency in take-offs and landings.

This flight was a consolidation for Tom. During this phase, a student pilot reviews his take-offs and landings, and thus becomes more proficient in this most critical phase of flying.

Having confidence in Tom's abilities, I told him that I would let him have the control of the aircraft throughout the mission, and would take over the controls only when I wanted to teach him something, or to correct any mistakes he might make.

Everything Appeared Fine

We flew in and made our first landing. It was not bad, so I instructed Tom to "go-around" — the term used to indicate a take-off immediately after landing. Tom responded by pushing the throttles all the way up to full power. The plane became a pack of "roaring power," sharply accelerating towards take-off speed.

As our aircraft broke the ground into the air, Tom selected the lever for landing gears up. He was doing "pretty well" and followed the proper procedure meticulously.

Relaxed, I looked outside, and watched other aircraft flying in the area. Suddenly I heard Tom's frantic voice.

"Sir, Overheat-Warning Light!"

Instantly, my attention went to the red blinking light which indicated our left engine was overheated. While I was concerned, it did not pose an alarming situation. I had encountered similar emergencies in the past and had coped with them successfully. Our right engine was enough to bring us in for a safe landing.

I took over the aircraft's controls and swiftly carried out the required procedures. I informed the control tower of our situation. They cleared us for a priority landing. Then I started the turn to land. At this point we were only about 250 feet above ground. Suddenly the blinking light turned steady, indicating that the left engine was on fire. Thick smoke entered the cockpit.

Alarm! Fire!

I reached down and switched off the left engine immediately. The right engine's thrust still sustained our flight. I transmitted the emergency on the radio. Then something drastic happened.

The RPM on the right engine started dropping! We learned later this happened because of a malfunction of the fuel pump. The right engine could not produce enough power thrust to sustain our flight. There was no choice. I hastily shouted to my student on the intercom:

"Eject! Eject!"

But as I turned to make sure Tom was following my orders I could not believe my eyes. He had frozen. He was rigid and glassy eyed. A tumult of thoughts rushed through my mind. "Should I eject?"

There were only seconds left. If I left him, he would surely die if he did not eject too. We lost more altitude. Our speed depleted until we were very close to the "bare-minimum-parameter" which is required in order to make a successful ejection. I tried once again to jolt Tom by yelling through the intercom "Eject! Eject!" Then I made hand signals to him, commanding him, thinking that perhaps the intercom had shorted out. All to no avail. He just stared ahead.

Split Second Decision

In order to save Tom's life, I decided to force-land the aircraft on a huge field which I could see in front of us. Let me explain. Jet aircrafts are not designed, nor recommended, for forced landing on an unprepared surface. Only a surface of asphalt or concrete, the kind used for runways, is safe to land this type of plane.

Imagine yourself speeding in a car on a highway at 125 M.P.H. Suddenly, the highway ends. You cannot use your breaks. You have in front of you uneven ground, full of bumps, trees, fences, and small ditches. You might rate your chances of survival as 0 to none. This is the reason jet aircrafts are not "recommended" for attempts at forced landings on unprepared surfaces.

I called in my intention of force-landing our aircraft. All other aircraft flying in the area listened to my emergency call on their radios. They thought I was crazy to try to attempt such a maneuver. Frankly, I thought so too. But it was a "roll of the dice." Our lives on one side, death on the other. I took the gamble.

As I followed the required procedures I was icy calm. Under such critical conditions, my calmness might sound exaggerated or even conceited. But believe me, it is the truth. Since we had only flown for fifteen minutes the fuel tanks were still full. I was scared that the aircraft might explode. In retrospect, I cannot believe that I was able to perform so well, and that I wasn't panicked.

There wasn't enough height to maneuver the aircraft in order to align it with the most ideal area, as I turned into a landing approach. I lowered the landing gears (wheels) praying that nothing would go wrong with their operation. Since I was manipulating the plane by sheer luck, I could not be positive of anything going right.

When the lights came on in the cockpit indicating gear (wheels down) and locked, I "Thanked Heaven!" It was a smooth touch-down, contrary to my expectations, but we did get some severe jolts from the uneven and bumpy ground. Finally I brought the aircraft to a halt. My student and I were still alive!

I informed the Control Tower of our successful landing. The aircraft was still in one piece. But the Control Tower shouted on the radio for us to abandon the aircraft because of the danger of fire and explosion... "Get away! Get away as soon as possible. Danger. Danger!"

Suddenly Tom Woke Up

Funniest thing. I was still in this struggle between life and death, but as I turned to look at Tom, he had already unstrapped himself from the seat, and had disconnected his radio leads and oxygen hose. Before I could switch off the equipment, he had abandoned ship, and was running down the field as fast as he could go.

Seeing him do this in that grim moment, I could not resist smiling and saying to myself. "I wish he had shown the same agility when I commanded him to eject!" But I was very happy as I climbed out. I had met death and defeated it. I now embraced life with new understanding.

Lessons From A Miracle

Three things I learned from this unusual incident:

1. **No matter how grave the situation**, if you keep your wits about you, have faith in God, and in yourself and your abilities, the chances are extremely bright that you will come out a winner. You will often be able to **help those of less ability — as you help yourself.**

2. **"Fortune favors the prepared mind."** I believe it. The incident of our forced landing proved it. It was compulsory for us (pilots) to attend daily "emergency meetings" held to brush up on the procedures we might have to carry out during a flight emergency. Most of us, including me, thought of it as a boring routine. But I learned the dividends, the value, of being prepared, **all the time.**

3. **There may be a risk** in trying something entirely new, but if you have faith in yourself, in your God, and you have the backing of your intuition, the risk is worth it. **Go for it.**

Magic Flying Carpets

It is a long time since I ceased pursuing my career as a pilot. I have now "flown" to the field of entrepreneurism in the United States. But I remember the lessons I learned from that forced landing and now apply them in my business and my new life.

Since my family in Pakistan manufactures gorgeous oriental rugs, my business here is importing and selling them. They are the exquisite handmade, fine carpets, originally created only for Rajahs, Rulers, and Kings (our name, Shah, means king).

The legends say our beautiful rugs were actually used for flying long ago! So my business card is a tiny "flying carpet." My winner's edge is the highest quality products, plus the secrets I have learned from the very successful people all over the world who buy my rugs.

My business education has been obtained in this unique manner. I have learned from those who have "made it big." Each of my teachers has flown to the heights of success, starting out from ground zero in humble backgrounds.

As in flying, where we pilots learn about using the jet streams above the earth to increase our speed and power, I have used the force of the knowledge of the most successful.

Some of this knowledge I acquired free, by meeting successful people through my family connections in Pakistan and the United States. Some of my knowlege came by purchasing seminars, books, albums, videos, and the time of the best teachers I could find. I consider each one a sound investment. I have paid as much as $2,000 for a one hour consultation. Here are some of the proven concepts I have learned.

Success Operators Manual

These are three powerful concepts that will turn over the engines of your mind, and get you moving on the runway to increased profits:

Concept #1. Make sure the product or service you offer to people is of the highest quality. Remember, a better product or service, promoted and advertised equally (against an inferior one) will always win in the long run.

Critically analyse your product or service. Get the opinion of friends and relatives who really care for your business. If your wares are not up to the mark, you owe it to yourself and your future clients to make a change for the better. Then you will always have the "Winner's Edge."

Concept #2. Widen your horizons. See your business as a real profit center. Approach the marketing of your materials from a different angle. Make a list of all the things you can do with your business to make it more profitable without making further cash investments.

You can think of many. Here is one; tap into the customer list of other businesses that are compatible to yours. Let's say you sell very expensive imported vases. Approach a furniture store that sells expensive furniture which is compatible to your vases. Cut a deal with them. You give them a part of your profits if they let you use their customer list. You might even have them mail out your material with their next mailing. You create a whole new market for yourself, which did not exist before.

Here is another one; reverse the above situation. Find a business which again is compatible to yours, and offer them the use of your customer list. You receive a share of their profits. You predetermine the deal with them in advance.

To go further, license the above concept to other businesses. Show them how to do it for a fee. The opportunities are unlimited in these joint ventures. Stretch your imagination.

Concept #3.   Recently the manager of a donut shop engaged me for a business consultation. He wanted to increase the volume of his business. The suggestion I gave him sounds simple, but it has brought him fantastic results.

This is what I asked him to do: Write a personal letter to all the businesses in your community. Offer them a tour of your donut store. Show them how donuts are made. Involve them, even let them try their hands at it. To make the effort of their visiting you worth while, and as a courteous gesture, offer them a free donut and cup of coffee at the end of the tour. Treat them royally. Be sure they have fun.

My client was rather skeptical, but he did mail seventy letters.   Eleven businesses, including schools, colleges, and banks responded. Most of them visited in groups.

The store manager made many new friends

who are now his permanent customers. He increased his business tremendously just by using this one simple concept. He has done the same thing many times since with different lists. Each time he ends up with new friends and customers. You can apply this same idea in your business. People will always appreciate your business more if you educate them in it. Try it, it works!

Your U.S.P.

Equip your business advertising campaign, no matter how large or small with U.S.P. — Unique Selling Proposition. What is it? A noted advertising man, Rosser Reeves, explained it in his book Reality in Advertising. U.S.P. is the hidden secret of literally thousands of the most successful business campaigns. U.S.P. is a precise term. Much money is frittered away by businesses because 90% do not know how the concept works.

1. Spell out a specific benefit that your product or service renders to the consumer. Example: If you are a manufacturer, wholesaler or retailer of cameras, you could point out the benefit, "Capture the most precious, colorful moments of your life with digital precision."

2. Your proposition must be unique either of brand, or design. It must be a claim that is not being made, or cannot be made by your competitors. When pointing out uniqeness, keep in mind it must be of importance to the consumer, or it will not serve your desired purpose.

Take the example of the camera. Let's say it does not require a flash attachment. This uniqueness would certainly benefit the consumer. They will not have to go through the aggravation of attaching the flash. The customer also saves money on batteries since your camera does not need them. So the unique benefits are savings, and convenience.

3. Make a strong proposition, one that becomes almost irresistible, so that the customer cannot pass it up. For our camera let's say, "Free, two rolls of color film when you buy your camera before May 30th. We will even pay for the film developing. See for yourself that you own one of the greatest cameras in the world. Try our camera for 30 days. *You will love it!* ^ If you are not satisfied, return it for a complete refund, and you may still keep your beautiful pictures."

Would you give this camera a try? I am sure I would. I urge you to apply U.S.P. in every ad and promotional campaign!

Test Flights

It is pathetic that so many businesses fail because they never test their advertisements. They are not able to find out exactly how well their ads are doing. When we skip this essential rule, we may never realize that the ads we think are the greatest, are far from finding that magic carpet in the mind of our customers.

The ad man may only satisfy our egos. The copy reads "I am wonderful." We forget the purpose of our advertisement: to show the customer we have what they need and want. We allow "ad men" to write "cutesy" ads, or let them merely blazen the name of our company. Believe me, your customer does not care one iota about your company, how long you have been in business, or how much money you make.

The only opinion that counts is that of the customer. If your ads are not giving you the expected response, don't delude yourself into thinking that it is something else, and not the lack of benefits and offers in your ads that are responsible.

Low Response Means The Ad Is Not Effective

Experiment carefully. Make changes in headlines, list benefits. Post your results. Learn the responsive chord by testing and recording each ad, each headline, claim, benefit, and descriptive body copy. You can increase the response to your advertising at least 10 times by this method.

Customers Zero In On Their Own Needs & Wants

Serve them. Help them. Make a significant improvement in their lives. Offer solutions to customer's problems. An amusing ad may get a chuckle, but people buy when the ad offers bene-fits. Remember, to sell is to serve. Customer's desires are Enlightened Self-Interest. Like the jet streams in the sky, if you will fly with the custom-ers needs, your business will zoom.

Success Flying Rules

a.   Always keep prospects in mind when crafting your ad. Put yourself into the buyer's shoes, and fly with their jet stream of self interest.
b.   Avoid crafting ads that say "We are wonderful" - cutesy without offering U.S.P.
c.   Test, Test, Test. Tabulate your results.
d.   Remember the wise saying: **"Advertising is the mother of commerce."**

Find A Business Co-Pilot

Top pilots do not seek the advice of the ignorant or unprepared. Aristotle said, "Man is a social ani-mal." We all need friends. But choose yours carefully. True friends are compassionate, under-standing, loving and altruistic. In my country they say, "Point out your friend to me, and I will tell you what you are."

The great qualities come with maturity. Suc-cessful people are not charlatans who try to im-press people by flaunting their wealth. Real suc-cessful people are those who have not only accu-mulated material wealth, but have the character-istics of strong character, spirit, honesty, humbleness, tenacity, steadfastness, and dynamic love for mankind. These qualities are the jet fuels of life.

Real friends win the heart of multitudes with their charismatic courageous personalities. Watch for these giants. Listen to their every sentence. Read what they write, ask for their assistance, even if you must wait for months to reach them. As Benjamin Franklin, that wise advertising man said, "Experience keeps an expensive school. A fool will learn in no other."

But understand, while such Captains of Business will be of enormous help, they are busy. Many seek them. So listen earnestly. Apply what they suggest. Do not expect them to stand on your shoulder to watch you or to do it for you. Do not be like Tom, running for his life. Remember to thank those who help you. Not for their sake, but for your own.

When you find a mentor, be discreet in your approach. Do not be impertinent, or take advantage of their politeness and patience. Be sincere, respectful and appreciative. You will then always be accepted with "open arms."

Your Flight Plan to Success

Lao Tsze, the mentor of Confucius, said, **"If you can see things in the seed, that is genius."**

When you have learned something you think others can benefit from, share your ideas with those who earnestly and truly seek your help. Each time you help others, you plant seeds of your own success. The tree of life pictured in my beautiful" flying" carpets depicts this wonderful growth theme.

Remember: *The destination of being a millionaire may not satisfy you. Helping even a fraction of a million people* **will certainly do so.**

BRUCE GIVNER, ESQ.
Sanger, Grayson, Givner & Booke
16633 Ventura Blvd., 6th Floor
Encino (Los Angeles) Calif, 91436
(213) 277-2267   (818) 788-3720

Bruce Givner

Bruce Givner is a popular and exciting speaker. In 1986-7 the California CPA Society had Bruce speak on a nationally televised new tax law program (viewed by over 14,000 CPAs); at its own new tax law conference (2,000 CPAS); at their annual meeting in Vancouver (500 CPAs), as well as at their Tax Accounting Conference (3,000 CPAs).

He has wowed audiences for the Lumber Association of Southern California, Textile Association of Los Angeles, Dean Witter Reynolds, Inc., Textile Professions Club, Meeting Planners International, Chevron Dealers' Association and many other trade associations with his witty and wise presentations.

Bruce is the author, or co-author of four books: <u>Maximizing Pension Deductions for Owners of Closely Held Business</u>, and <u>The Role of Small CPA Firms in Taking Closely Held Corporations Public</u>, both published by the California CPA Foundation; <u>Tax Practice in California</u> (California Continuing Education of the Bar); and <u>Tax Problems of Fiduciaries</u> (American Law Institute-American Bar Association).

The Wall Street Journal, United States Tax Court and California Court of Appeals have cited Bruce Givner as a tax expert.

Bruce Givner is a graduate of U.C.L.A., Columbia University Law School, and N.Y.U. (Graduate Tax Program.) He has been an adjunct tax professor at Golden Gate University and the University of San Diego.

Shake 'Em Up

By Bruce Givner, Esq.

*"Always do right. This will gratify some people
and astonish the rest."*

- Mark Twain

What do MOVERS, SHAKERS AND CHANGE
MAKERS have in common?

<u>CREATIVITY</u>. Webster's defines "creative" as
"having the quality of something created rather
than imitated." "Imaginative" is a synonym. How
do you use creativity in your business? In your
life? There is always a way. Can you imagine a
more deathly topic than tax law? That is my
profession.

When I tell people I am a "tax attorney," they

are repulsed: "Oh, you stuff dead animals and put them on plaques. That's disgusting!" "No, ma'am" I reply. "That's taxidermy."

How To Use Creativity

Creativity is important in my profession in at least two ways: (1) Tax planning and (2) Marketing my services. Your business is probably not much different. So let us examine one use of creativity in tax planning.

The following is a fact situation reported by Leo Rosten: An IRS agent walked into Feinberg's Fancy Deli and asked for the owner. "I am Milton Feinberg," said one of the men behind the counter. The IRS agent flashed his identification. "I have a question about your income tax returns, Mr. Feinberg."

They sat down at a corner table. The IRS agent opened his briefcase and pulled out a folder. He spread its contents before Mr. Feinberg and said:

"I call your attention to this section — Professional Expenses, tax-deductible."

"My expenses are very big," said Mr. Feinberg.

"But not <u>this big</u>," said the IRS agent. "Look, right here, under 'Business Expenses,' you list five trips to Israel!"

"Right."

"Five trips to Israel? You call those <u>business</u> expenses?!"

"Certainly."

"How can a small delicatessen justify — "

"What do you mean 'justify?'" Mr. Feinberg retorted in a huff: **"We deliver!"**

Some call it thinking outside the square. Some call it creativity. Edison said "it" is a direct result of laziness.

I'm Lazy

Who wouldn't be lazy in the face of:

3,000 pages in the Internal Revenue Code. The law as written by congress.

9,000 Pages of IRS Regulations. The IRS' view of what the law means.

100,000 Pages of Revenue Rulings and related material. The IRS' view of the results in specific fact situations.

600,000 Pages of cases decided by the U.S. Tax Court.

And on and on. Ad infinitum. Ad nauseum. All that authority to consult. How do you know what to do? How do you advise clients? What do you tell rich people - who are paying you $250.00 per hour - about structuring their businesses and personal estates to limit their tax liabilities?

GIVNER'S RULE: IT'S PERMITTED UNLESS PROHIBITED

Challenge: Many situations are not clearly covered by the law. What advice do you give?

Status Quo: Some tax lawyers are known as

"aggressive." Some are known as "conservative." Some are known by a more technical description; "wishy-washy."

Problem: Clients want a straightforward, easily understood answer to their questions. H. L. Mencken said "There usually is an answer to any problem: Simple, clear, and wrong." Both extremes of advice — aggressive and conservative — have their own shortcomings.

Most Aggressive: If I say, "The IRS will never figure it out. Your chances of getting audited are less than one percent," the one client in one hundred will forget any cautionary statements I made. He'll sue me when the audit proves unsuccessful.

Most conservative: If I say, "Well, the IRS wouldn't like that if they figured it out," clients will view me as "gutless." They would have saved money by calling the IRS with the question.

Uncreative Solution: Describe the range of alternatives. In response to the most conservative's fears: So what. The IRS does not pay me. The fact that they do not like "it" (whatever it is) does not make it illegal. In response to the most aggressive, bull-headed approach: True. Your chances of getting audited are — in general — less than one percent. But that one time may cost three times as much money as paying the taxes in the first place.

If you decide to follow the most aggressive approach make sure you understand the difference between tax avoidance and tax evasion: 5 years and $50,000 per count.

Describing the range of alternatives is the

easy, partial answer. What people will do depends upon the tone of voice I use in delivering the message.

Most people do not have the emotional stamina to suffer through a losing audit. They hate risk. Therefore they will select the conservative approach.

That Is What the IRS Is Counting On

The IRS Collections Division is not fun to deal with — especially when they are in a feeding frenzy. One time I accompanied a client to a meeting with an IRS Collections Division Agent. We met in the agent's office. As with most government offices, it was sparsely furnished. Behind his desk were two items: An American flag; and an IRS "For Sale" sign and seizure notice.

The agent's eyes narrowed into slits that made him look like Clint Eastwood. He pointed behind his desk and looked straight at my client:
"We're here to decide which of these is going to end up sticking in your front lawn."
Creative Solution: If I only describe alternatives people will be confused. They want advice. They want a recommended course of action. So when the legal course of action is unclear I include: *"Forgetting for a moment that I am a tax lawyer, if it were my money and I were in your situation I'd..."*
Otherwise, clients will not have received what

they consider to be helpful. And that is what gives tax lawyers a bad name.

The Value Of Advice

Some of you are surprised to hear that some tax lawyers have a bad name? Consider the following true story:

Two wealthy industrialists, Sam Phillips and Joe Gutenberg were traveling across the country in a hot air balloon. They drifted for several days. The clouds were so thick they could not see the ground. They could not tell if they were in Iowa, or Idaho.

"Let's let some air out of the balloon," Sam suggested. "Then we can glide down through the cloud cover and ask someone on the ground where we are."

Joe agreed. The balloon descended. The clouds separated to reveal the earth below. A man — Irving Lipshitz — was walking along carrying a briefcase. He saw the balloon above him. Sam called down, "Can you tell us where we are?"

Irving studied the two men in the balloon. He put his briefcase down, cupped his hands and shouted: **"You're in a hot air balloon!"**

Sam was puzzled. Joe said, "That guy is a tax lawyer."

"How do you know?" asked Sam. "Because of the briefcase?"

"No," Joe blurted out. "In my business I deal with many tax lawyers. It's not the briefcase."

"Oh," moaned Sam." I know. It's because of the 3 piece suit."

"No," replied Joe. "It's because what he told us was absolutely correct and utterly worthless."

Creative Clients

Having a reputation for creatively applying the law is a great marketing advantage. However, I cannot claim to have originated all the creative approaches I now employ on behalf of clients. Some are generated by the clients themselves.

In 1981 Congress passed the E.R.T.A. (Economic Recovery Tax Act of 1981). Perhaps the most important change in the law was the introduction — principally for estate tax purposes — of the unlimited marital deduction.

My wealthiest client, Joe, called me about the impact of the new law on his estate. Joe was, at the time, 74 years old and unmarried. "I've been reading about this new unlimited marital deduction," he said. "I'm going to marry my 26 year old secretary. This way I can leave everything to her free of death taxes."

Tax lawyers are not trained psychologists. However, given the long-standing relationship I have with Joe, I had to venture a personal comment about his proposed plan.

"You know, Joe, at your age, having sex could be fatal."

Joe shrugged. "If she dies... she dies."

Creative Marketing

Now that we have carefully considered the use of creativity in solving legal problems, let us discuss its use in marketing legal services.

Challenge: In 1977 Tax lawyers were in great demand. Highly paid, highly respected, well known in the business community. And snooty. That was the situation when I started practicing law. I thought, "How am I going to compete with these folks? They are all smarter and better known" And imperious.

Status Quo: CPAs supply most new work for tax lawyers. Therefore, most tax lawyers do not charge CPAs for advice. Reason: give the CPAs "freebies" and they will refer clients to you.

Problem: CPAs would call me one, two or even three times for a "freebie." Then they would not call again.

"Why did you stop calling me?" I would ask. The CPA would sheepishly respond: "I was not able to refer you enough business to justify the time you spent with me."

Solution: Don't worry. When you have questions I will give you the help - and bill you for it. You need not worry about referring me business."

Aftermath: Some CPAs were shocked at the idea of paying for what had been free advice. But the busiest ones — the ones who wanted the right legal answers, not the free answers — loved it. By paying they did not have to think about referrals. Here is the surprise. Who gets more referrals? Me — or lawyers who still give "freebies"?

No scientific study has been made. But it appears I get more referrals by charging CPAs than most tax lawyers get by giving free advice. Why? Because tax lawyers giving "freebies" do not give good advice? Not really. People are conscientious. No tax lawyer purposefully slights a "freebie" because it really is not "free". It is current payment for future referrals. Then why? Because CPAs are liberated from an obligation to refer business? Maybe. Because CPAs place more value on something they pay for? Perhaps. Because paying gives CPAs the right to demand the highest quality service? The right to complain? Perhaps. It is hard to complain about the timeliness or quality of a "freebie." Because of all of these reasons? Yes. And more.

The biggest additional reason I get more referrals is humor. (People think I am funny looking.)

A Funny Thing Happens On The Way To The Tax Forum

Creative marketing of tax law requires the use of humor. What is your image of a tax lawyer? Austere. Three piece suit. Thick glasses. Rich. Nerdy. Certainly a sense of humor is not the first trait that jumps to mind. In fact, when it comes to tax lawyers, the humor is more often about them, than by them. One CPA gave the following example: "What do you get when you cross the Godfather with a tax attorney?" "An offer you can't understand."

Another CPA complained to me long and bitterly about a tax attorney colleague of mine. Then he asked me: "What is black and brown and looks good on a tax attorney?" "I don't know," I foolishly replied. "A doberman."

Clients have a different perspective on tax attorneys: "What do you call 600 lawyers at the bottom of a lake?" "I don't know." "A good start."

Using humor separates me from the stereotypical tax attorney. It is creative. It is also dangerous. People thinking of taxes are serious. They do not want a part-time comic helping them with a situation involving thousands, hundreds of thousands, or even millions of dollars in taxes. Therefore, I do not tell jokes. In fact, people who hear me speak assure me that nothing I say is funny.

Henny Youngman heard me speak once. I was flattered that he sought me out afterwards to pay what I hoped would be a compliment. "You certainly have a ready wit," he said. "Tell me when it's ready."

Since I do not tell jokes well, I do not tell them at all. Instead, I let my clients do the talking. Everyone says truth is funnier than fiction. That may be true. But fiction has an advantage. Mark Twain said the difference between truth and fiction is that fiction must make sense.

Quo Vadis?

Many interesting stories flow out of an area of tax law that is literally the deadliest: Estate Planning. Husband and wife were in my office for almost two hours. I described, in great detail, the government's impact on their estate plan. We discussed saving death taxes by using the unlimited marital deduction and the unified credit. I described avoiding probates and conservatorships through the use of a living trust.

Finally we came to what would happen to their property after they were both dead. I asked about the children. The father said: "My children can have whatever filters through my kidneys." Parents reveal themselves when doing estate planning. Another client, talking about the same topic, how to leave property for his children, advised: "If you leave your children liquid assets, they will drink them."

Some people, when considering their own mortality, grow apprehensive. Then, when I tell them the cost of two pour-over wills and a living trust to avoid probates and a conservatorship, they become glassy-eyed. To mitigate that problem, I offer estate planning clients a free money back guarantee. "Our wills are free if used within 48 hours." That guarantee has been cost-effective. So far no one has taken me up on it.

Conclusion.

You must be creative to be a MOVER, SHAKER AND CHANGE MAKER. Shake people up. Like the three trained professionals who met to discuss creativity's use in their respective professions: A doctor, a management consultant, and a lawyer.

They talked for hours. At one point the doctor claimed that creativity had always been used in medicine, so medicine is the oldest profession: "In the very first book of the bible God took a rib from Adam to make Eve. That's a kind of surgery. Surgery is medicine. So medicine is the oldest."

The management consultant was furious at the doctor's misinformed analysis. He shouted back: "You're wrong. In the very first sentence of the Bible it says that out of chaos God created order. That is what management consultants do when they go into a business; create order out of chaos. So management consulting is the oldest profession."

"You are both wrong," said the tax attorney. **"Who do you think created the chaos?"**

JOE D. BATTEN
Batten, Batten, Hudson & Swab, Inc.
820 Keosauqua Way
Des Moines, IA 50309
(515) 244-3176 (515) 285-7088

Joe Batten

In addition to his numerous honors in the field of management, Joe Batten is known throughout the world as the DEAN OF SA-LESTRAINERS.

He is the founder and Chairman of the Board of Batten, Batten, Hudson & Swab, Inc., Des Moines, Iowa, a 30 year old management consulting firm engaged in creative management research, consulting film production, and educational services. Joe is a renowned consultant, philospher, speaker, trainer, film maker, and author. He is known world-wide as the author of Tough Minded Management *and such films as* Keep Reaching *and* Ask For the Order. *He has spoken over 2,000 times on motivation, selling and management. He is a charter member of the National Speakers Association Hall of Fame (CPAE.)*

Joe Batten is a renowned consultant and speaker in the United States and abroad. He has trained thousands in manage-ment, sales, and human relationship skills. His teachings are acclaimed as the proto-type for tomorrow's management. His philosophy advocates the development of the "Whole Person" and he and his colleagues have been heavily involved in counseling and speaking on "Whole Person Wellness" stress management. BBH&S is taking bold innovative steps in chemical dependency and wellness counseling and conducts definitive research and program presentations in corporations of all kinds. He is generally consid-ered to be the principal pioneer in the establishment of management philosophies, basic beliefs, and values as the basis of corporate cultures/climates. His book Tough Minded Management, *is and has been the leadership bible for several heads of state. Joe's advo-cates include H. Ross Perot, J. Willard Marriott, Berkeley Bedell, and other legendary executives.*

He has written numerous articles for national publications and has appeared on network television and radio programs as well as local television and radio. As an author, he has received wide acknowledgment from organizations throughout the world.

The Tough-Minded Visioneer

By Joe Batten, C.P.A.E.

Lose yourself in productive work -
in a way of excellence.
                    - Aristotle

The next decade will offer a mind-boggling array of opportunities. Those who reach out, search for, and welcome change will experience some wonderful things. Those who shrink pallidly and passively into a twilight of protecting the status quo will, in all likelihood, experience a good bit of misery.

    If you're a Visioneer — one who dares to dream

— here is a platter of tested techniques and truths. People like H. Ross Perot, Lee Iacocca, and Vince Lombardi have carved out patterns of success which illustrate the efficacy of these principles.

Dare To Dream and Stretch

While riding through the mountains in one of our Western states, I was paying close attention to the man driving me to the airport from a speech at one of our great Universities. He was a cheerful, ruddy faced, and highly intelligent Ph.D.

"Joe, if these people remember just one thing you said, it'll really change their lives. It will virtually <u>propel</u> them to success."

"What's that?" I inquired.

He smiled and said, "You challenged them to get rid all the "lousy apostrophe t's" in their vocabulary, that's what."

Since then, I've talked to a great many **"Movers and Shakers"** who are doing very well. Regrettably, I've talked to a <u>great many who have failed because of negative thinking.</u>

It's so important to realize that we not only BECOME WHAT WE THINK, but that we also BECOME WHAT WE SAY.

You see, the only way we can realistically and consistently purge our language of words like:

can't	don't
won't	shouldn't
wouldn't	hasn't
couldn't	didn't

and... "all those apostrophe t's," is to re-think, re-group, re-organize and re-sculpt the way we think. I'm challenging hundreds of organizations all over the world to eliminate all their apostrophe t's for just thirty days. It has been gratifying indeed to then, for instance, be stopped in an airport by a person who says something like this:

"It wasn't a piece of cake to make the change, but when I reached the point where most of what I thought and said was highly positive, all kinds of successes began to come my way. People are attracted by positive thinkers and talkers because such people are always much more positive and productive do'ers."

And... many variations of the above. In order to pull much of this together into an action planning blueprint for you, as a mover, shaker, and change maker, please note the Expective Life Planning Instrument which I have borrowed from my book, "Expectations and Possibilities" (Addison-Wesley, 1981).

After reading it once, please re-read it and re-read it and re-read it. I have been told that many times about the sixth time through a great feeling of direction, purpose, and focus begins to literally start the adrenaline pumping. Here it is:

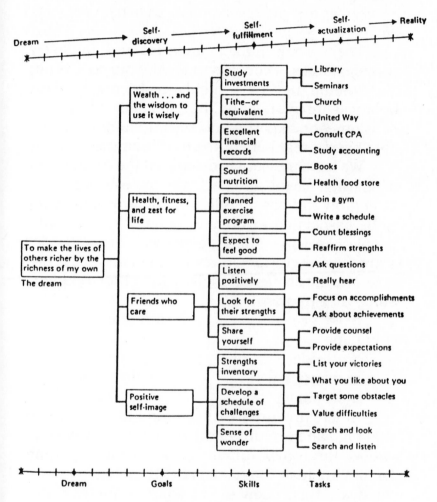

Expective life planning instrument.

After you have begun to find guidance and inspiration for yourself, please prepare copies to give to your colleagues and, <u>most importantly,</u> everyone with whom you'd like to be associated:

whether in your business, your school, your church, or any and every other dimension of your life.

These items make wonderful and endlessly varied sources of conversation. The purpose is not and should not be selfishly restricted to your business interests only: but somehow these discussions and experiments seem to almost invariably have a real benefit to your business.

We have previously discussed the practicality of sharing, caring and daring — to be aware of the strengths and possibilities of others. People <u>want</u> to be associated in business and otherwise with people like you. Many people who are potential stars in your group — but who don't know it yet — are almost ill, <u>emotionally</u> starved for relationships that nourish:

trust	self starting
hope	faith
gratitude	love
reassurance	reaffirmation
new vitality	

Americans are just beginning to understand that high and exciting earnings, expanding organizations and goal fulfillment stem directly from factors such as those we are discussing here. To illustrate this, allow me to share a quote or two each from two world class leaders. They are Mr. Konosuke Matsushita, Chairman of the Board of the fantastically successful Matsushita Industries, and Mr. Vince Lombardi whose leadership in sports was virtually without peer.

After Mr. Matsushita studied books like

"Tough-Minded Management" and "Beyond Management by Objectives" in the early sixties, he wrote me a letter in which he discussed what he called "The Secret of Success." One of his many powerful thoughts was this: *"There are many secrets of success, but the <u>most important</u> one, I think, is <u>looking at people's strong points</u> and an attitude of making the most of them."*

When you look at Matsushita's bottom line, the question "how <u>practical</u> can you get?" is obvious.

Vince Lomabardi truly understood the meaning of applied <u>mental toughness</u> and dared to shake the sports world with his own toughness of mind. When asked what the "secret" of the success of the Green Bay Packers was, he grinned and answered powerfully and simply: *"These guys love each other!"*

Do you think he was kidding? Was he referring to a soupy sort of sentimental love only? Was he impractical? He knew that the only way a team that was older, smaller, and slower than any other in professional football could win was to feel and apply superior **spirit, will,** and **effort.** Where do these qualities come from? The space between the ears!

They dreamed...

 They planned...

  They believed...

   They won!

You can, too.

How To Build a Professional Organization

If building a business is such a fine instrument of free enterprise, such an excellent method of achieving success, why all the failures? Why the dreams that seemingly go up in smoke? Sure! I know about some great successes, but there are <u>too many</u> failures.

There are more failures than there **should** be, but it is our intent here to focus precisely on how to maximize successes, how to build the kind of professional organization and managerial style that will endure, thrive and prosper.

Management, whether involved in a for-profit or non-profit organization, <u>always</u> deals in varying degrees and quantities with five resources: **People, Money, Materials, Time and Space.**

May I present to you fifty qualities of the professional manager and the professionally managed organization? They are stretching. They are tested and tough-minded. Adherence to these qualities and techniques have built some of the finest and enduring buinesses the world has ever seen. Here we go...

As an individual, the professional tough-minded manager:
   •Practices self-discipline in terms of legal and ethical rules of conduct. Knows that vigor, mental clarity and creativity are always products of self-discipline.

•Knows that developing and maintaining maximum fitness; physical, mental and spiritual, is crucial to mental health, excellent decision making, and full functioning.

•Enjoys life — and lets people know it! Has not time for gloomy, downbeat thinking and action.

•Has interests and activities which range widely with a prioritized focus on certain key areas. Knows that understanding the big picture sharpens understanding of specifics.

•Has either developed or is moving toward a strong personal faith. Knows that believing in a power greater than self is important in order to truly believe in self and in others.

•<u>Never</u> apologizes for a thing before doing it. But <u>does</u> apologize if he/she knows he/she has not done the very best. Knows that if you say, "I'll try..." and fail, you've met your objective. We prepare to succeed or fail with the words we use. We <u>become</u> what we <u>say!</u>

•Believes that negativism is <u>never</u> justified. Knows that since the word "negative" really means... "less than nothing," the only reality of anything is/are the present and potential strengths which are there.

•Always wants to know the <u>why</u> of a happening and supplies the <u>why</u> conscientiously to others.

•Thirsty for facts, but knows that variables often exceed constants, and is not hemmed in by them.

•Believes strongly in God, their fellow person, and themself.

•Retains a healthy <u>un</u>satisfaction with his/

her abilities as a communicator. Knows that mere "dialogue" is not enough, that real communication means "shared meaning — shared understanding."

•Cultivates an open, growing sense of wonder. Wants to constantly learn, savor, and experience new things.

•Goes right to the heart of problems. Focuses on <u>cause</u> not symptoms, on <u>bottom line</u>, not activity.

•Knows that diligent and productive <u>work</u> is at the heart of all good things.

•Seeks a broad and eclectic fund of knowledge about his objectives.

•Proud of the American way of life and seeks to enrich the lives of others.

•Seeks to acquire some new wisdom every day of their life.

•Strives for a balanced existence: of work, rest, play, and quality thinking.

•Believes in the wholesome, creative, and renewing power of humor and laughter.

•Satisfied with nothing less than full success as a whole person. Strives steadily to <u>exceed</u> him/herself.

•Takes work seriously but can laugh at self.

As a Manager, within their own team, the tough-minded PROFESSIONAL man or woman will:

•Insure that all team members know the what, where, when, who, how and above all — why of their roles and goals.

•Insure that all team members clearly understand the results expected of them.

•Insure that financial rewards are related closely to clearly understood results expectations.

•Live and exemplify the concept that the development of people, as a whole and in depth, pays real dividends to the success of the business.

•Insure that all team members meet performance commitments or leave the team.

•Make certain that the statement, "Management is of, by, about, and for PEOPLE" goes beyond lip service into reality.

•Know that all people will contribute and receive more if they are helped to develop clear feelings of purpose, direction, dignity, and expectations.

•Know that all team members must receive really excellent and thorough training and product knowledge.

•Strive to develop in all team members an awareness of the value of work to them.

•Believe in utilizing all modern high tech resources which are appropriate. But, always considers "high tech" secondary to "high touch."

•Exemplify that "the value of any organization is the sum of the values between the ears of its people."

•Provide an example that radiates positivism, purpose, direction, discipline, and care.

•Exemplify that technological tools and techniques are always more effective when used by people with mature conceptual wisdom.

•Provide an example that seems to say: STAY WITHIN SIGHT OF MY HEELS, AND WE'LL GET A LOT DONE — AND HAVE A LOT OF FUN — AND, YOU CAN'T DO MUCH OF ONE WITHOUT THE OTHER.

In our modern global community, it is crucial for the PROFESSIONAL manager/entrepreneur, who is a mover and shaker, to function effectively as a productive member of our society.

As A Member of Society, the man or woman who is committed to business professionalism will:

•<u>Live</u> integrity rather than just <u>talking</u> a good game.
•Carry his/her emphasis on results over into community and industrywide activities.
•Practice truth and candor widely and reflect <u>warmth</u> throughout the community.
•Have the courage to confront and grapple with issues that affect the quality of community life.
•Live the precepts contained in this series of tough-minded qualities.
•Illustrate "humanitarian" qualities.
•Seek to illustrate that applied integrity is at the core of all true social, political, and economic progress.
•Seek to strengthen the caliber of political and municipal officials rather than dwelling caustically on their weaknesses.

•Constantly seek to strengthen our society as a whole rather than to highlight its weaknesses.

•Move beyond just appointing a committee. Wants target dates set, objectives defined — then ACTION.

As you begin to truly conceptualize, formulate, and build a professional and profitable organization, it is vital to temper and saturate all parts of your enterprise and or unit with a commitment to SERVICE.

The Movers, Shakers and Change makers are tough minded visioneers. They understand what Jesus meant when He explained, ***"The one who would be greatest among you, must be servant of all."***

**Dottie Walters receives the
Certified Speaking Professional (CSP) designation
presented by Ty Boyd, past president of the
National Speakers Association.**

DOTTIE WALTERS, C.S.P.
Royal Publishing, Inc.
18825 Hicrest Road
P.O. Box 1120
Glendora, CA 91740
(818) 335-8069

Dorothy M. Walters, C.S.P.

Dottie Walters is unique. She began her long and illustrious career with no car, one rickety stroller, two babies, a borrowed typewriter and a high school education. There were no jobs. The country was in a recession when Dottie started down the long road. She put cardboard in her shoes and kicked the wheel back on the stroller each time it came off.

Today Dottie is a World Class Speaker, President of her International Speakers Bureau and Publisher of the largest newsmagazine in the world for Speakers. She had been honored three times by the National Speakers Association, with the Certified Speaking Professional designation, one of the first four United States women to receive it. She is a founding member of N.S.A., as well as the founding member and officer of the Greater Los Angeles N.S.A. Chapter. She has initiated and sold several businesses, all based on advertising and publishing. She is Executive Director of International Group of Agents and Bureaus.

She is president of four corporations, author, speaker, seminar leader, publisher of anthologies featuring outstanding speakers, poet, featured in many TV and radio shows, newspaper and magazine articles, books and cassettes worldwide. Her first book, Never Underestimate the Selling Power of a Woman *is in its 14th edition.*

Dottie and Bob Walters have three children; an attorney, a drama teacher, and the manager of their International Speakers Bureau. Dottie and Bob live in Glendora, California.

The New Women Buyers are Movers and Shakers

By Dottie Walters, C.S.P.

*"What Women say is nonsense?
He who does not listen is a fool."*
-African Bemba

When I began speaking to promote my advertising sales business, women bought groceries, clothes, simple things, but if they ventured into the area of large purchases they had to "ask their husbands."

One of our advertising accounts was a local newspaper's circulation department. Our job, to sell subscriptions. We surveyed the women and learned they thought they could not spend $3.75 — the annual price, without permission.

We designed advertising copy that explained the value of the newspaper, the coupons, the bargains in classified, all for just over a penny a day. Our headline asked if it was o.k. with their husbands for them to invest that much for such great value. It worked.

Magazines were full of articles then advising women to "Let the man be the boss," and "Don't let him know how smart you are, or he will leave you." It wasn't so long ago that women were seldom promoted to managerial jobs. Few owned businesses. Since high paying jobs were out of the question for women, keeping the husband happy was an economic necessity.

Things Have Changed

The latest U.S. census reports state five million wives earn more than their husbands. Of every six new businesses opened in the U.S., five are begun by women entrepreneurs. Of course not all of them succeed, but just as many of these female-run companies make it as those headed by men.

Women are building business, career, and political empires. Golda Meir and Amelia Earhart opened the doors. Margaret Thatcher and Mrs. Fields of chocolate chip cookie fame, led the parade through. Typical examples are Mary Kay Ash and Estee Lauder, who began their enterprises on their kitchen table and now run multi-million dollar companies.

With purses heavy with money, Women Buyers are stepping out to make their own decisions. Some salesmen are as confused by the Woman Buyer as Sigmund Freud. At the end of Freud's long career of studying the human mind, he said disparingly, **"I don't know what these women WANT!"**

Wayne Gretsky, the famous Canadian hockey player, says his father told him, "Aim where the puck is GOING." As I speak to sales people, I love to explain to them what the Woman Buyer wants, where she is going. Freud may not have known, but we women do know what we want.

Latest Estimates

Women influence 84% of all cars purchased today. Forty one percent of automobile sales are made by the Woman Buyer who buys alone. Sixteen percent are purchased by men alone. The balance of automobile sales are man/woman purchase situations.

Women buy trucks, tractors, fleets of cars. Last year 4.6 million cars were delivered to women who made the purchase by themselves. They spent 46 billion dollars in this one area. However, what these figures do not reveal is how many dealerships insulted the Women Buyers and drove them away into the arms of those who treated them with respect.

Now She Has the Money

Smart salespeole get in step with the new Woman Buyer, while others pull boners that drive her out of their businesses. Could it be that some salespeople are like the Biblical brothers who had sold their little brother Joseph into slavery?

Years later these same brothers came, hat in hand, to ask the king for food during a famine. They were aghast to learn little brother Joseph was now the king's top advisor, the very person they must deal with to obtain what they wanted.

"What do we say?" they quavered.

My programs around the world help salespeople to know what to say to the new Woman Buyer. Let's review here how women feel and what they want. Let's look at what is going on the new Woman Buyers mind.

How Do They See Themselves?

Ben Bidwell, Vice Chairman of Chrysler Corporation, reported to the press recently that most women feel automobile salespeople have long ignored and bullied them.

A new Canadian survey found the adjective most women who work use to describe themselves is "brave." Do you see your woman buyer as courageous?

She is still a housewife. Often a single parent.

She doesn't play golf, she moonlights on the housework. Her recreation is taking the kids to Little League, band practice or the Girl Scouts.

She wants to tell the mechanic herself that her car goes "kaplunkata." She does not like to have to tell it to a middleman. She doesn't want to be laughed at. She wants it fixed. The first time. And she wants a ride home while it is being fixed, please.

Perhaps all of those assertiveness seminars have taken hold.

The Ladies Home Journal advertised recently, "When the new Woman Buyer shops, she has a sharp eye for performance and value. She's a tough, demanding consumer - one no business can afford to miss. She drives a hard bargain."

How can salespeople shift gears to work with her?"

Creative Ideas

Women Buyers may be tough customers, but there are some ideas you can use. Tips that work. Ways to please them, have them buy from you again and again, and have them recommend you to their friends.

Automobile dealers are featuring comfortable lounges in both the sales and auto repair departments. Some offer continental breakfasts to working people who bring their car in for work in the morning - delivering them to the job in shuttles.

Fifty percent of most dealership revenue is derived from the repair department. Catering to the Woman Buyer's needs is profitable. She is not nearly as apt to fix the car herself.

Some automobile dealers have set up special show rooms, and car repair waiting rooms, with carpets, drapes, refreshments and comfortable chairs. A box of toys and children's books wait for young fry in a teasure chest. Women buyers enjoy these amenities. Tim Roth, Colorado Chevrolet dealer says, "Two or Three customers a day come in, just for our new special showroom."

Dealers invite business women to catered luncheons at the dealership where their opinions are invited. Some take pictures of these women buyers in the new cars, and use them with their endorsements (and a plug for her business) in the dealer's advertisements.

In California, a Cadillac dealer has successfully used an amusing radio commercial which features two women talking in a restaurant. Their conversation topic is their choice of color for their new Allante. (The Allante currently sells for $55,000.) Should they choose gold, pearl, grey or wine?

A man leans over from the next table and interrupts.

"You dollies don't want one of those high priced babies. See my car out front? Choose a cheap car in a drab color. That's what I do. By the way, I like good looking broads. Come on over to the all night laundry across the street. I might let you fill out a job application."

One woman replies, "Your car would never fit my image. I am a Doctor." The other agrees, "Nor mine, I am a Supreme Court Judge."

The man beats a hasty retreat.

Of course not all of the new Women Buyers are judges or doctors, but it is a fact that more women than men are entering colleges and more women than men today are qualifying as professionals. Yet some salespeople still think of women as the silent partner of the man buyer. **T'aint so.**

Three Women Go Out to Buy a Car

A number of years ago, when Mary Kay Ash (Mary Kay Cosmetics) was beginning her business, she had a dream. She wanted to show her salespeople how to set and achieve goals. She planned to earn the money for a new car by her birthday, and to buy it on that day. She studied the various makes and decided on just the right car for her business needs.

Finally, on her birthday she was ready with the money. She knew exactly which car she wanted and felt she could pay for. She was excited as she walked into the automobile lot with her checkbook in hand.

A young man came towards her. Without asking her any questions he said, "I am just going to lunch. Why don't you go and get your husband, and come back later in the afternoon."

"But it is my birthday. I want to buy a car now," she protested. "Could you call the salesmanager please?"

"Oh, no," the salesman said. "The salesmanager is already out to lunch. Besides, we don't like to show cars to women by themselves. It is a waste of time."

Mary Kay, who is a beautiful blonde, turned and walked sadly out of the lot. Across the street was another car dealer. In the show window was displayed a gorgeous, expensive car. She walked across and looked longingly at it.

A young man stepped out. "You are right!" he smiled." That beautiful car just matches your hair!"

She shook her head. "I wanted to buy a less expensive car today on my birthday. I don' t think I can afford this one."

This dealership had evidently been listening to my "SMI" cassette about the meaning of red roses, the "SEVEN SECRETS OF SELLING TO WOMEN." It includes the story of the goddess Venus who sent Cupid out to ask mortals to be quiet when she was making love. He gave passersby one red rose, so goes the legend.

The red rose signifies, "Shhhh. Love going on here. It is a secret." Romans hung a red rose over the dining table, meaning, "Anything we say here will be held in confidence. You can trust us. Love going on here." Catholic confessionals had red roses painted on the ceilings. "Shhh. Love going on here. A secret." That is how the term Sub-Rosa came into being.

"Your birthday!" The car salesman grinned at Mary Kay. "We keep red roses here for lady buyers who come in on their birthday! Come on inside, I have a red rose for you to help you celebrate. Let me be your buyer's assistant. I'll help you to own the car of your dreams. You deserve the best. You can drive it home today."

He did. She did.

Mary Kay Ash now uses fleets of cars for her saleswomen.

If only that first young man had asked a few questions. If only he had appreciated that Woman Buyer instead of depreciating her.

Perhaps you are thinking that his attitude toward his Woman Buyer is a thing of the past — a long time ago. Listen to these two stories. Both occurred within the past 12 months.

Opportunity Walks In

Robin Westmiller, a successful Glendale, California business woman, walked into a dealership recently to buy a van. Her two small children were in tow. She had chosen this car dealer because they are close to her home and would be convenient for service and repairs.

"Honey, you better go home and get your husband," the salesman told her. "You won't understand about the mechanical things on the cars, or the terms of the sale."

Robin protested, "But my husband is not

mechanical, I am! Besides, the van is for my own business. I earned the money, I am buying it myself."

"Sure, I know. You'd better go home and get your husband. We're only allowed to work with the decision maker," the salesman insisted. He did not ask her about her business. How she would use the car. Nor did he get her name or phone number for follow up. He lost her.

Robin walked out, drove to another dealership, and bought her car.

How much did the first dealership spend in advertising to bring in a customer? What does it cost to lose not only the initial sale, but the lucrative repair business as well?

Robin said, "They couldn't believe I was mechanical, owned my own business, or am smart enough to make a deal. They depreciated me. I will never go back there again."

Sandra Van, a very successful publicist, had her Cadillac in the garage, so her brother-in-law took her automobile shopping in his older car. This time the salesman ignored her. He would not answer any of her questions. He laughed at her, and gave all of his attention to the non-buyer, the brother-in-law.

Sandra finally gave up in disgust and drove to the next town where she was assisted by an intelligent, interested salesperson. That is where she bought her car.

Tips On Selling the Woman Buyer

1. Look genuinely pleased to see her. Don't act as if you lost the straw pull, and are forced to be the one to wait on her.

Once, on a trip to Mexico, a young teen ager with his little sister beside him came up to me on the street. "Hello!" he smiled. **"I am the one you have been searching for!"**

I was astounded. "What do you mean?" I asked. He had nothing in his hands to sell. All around us vendors were calling out their wares of sarapes, food, birds, all kinds of things for sale.

"Look at this, lady," he grinned. He pulled out a clear plastic vial of opals from his pocket." These match your eyes.They are full of fire too. You deserve them. My sister and I dug them out of the mountain early this morning. I want you to have them."

I bought all he had. He was right. The excitement, the love, the enthusiasm in his eyes were what I was waiting for. We all hope to find an interested salesperson.

2. Smile. Some salesmen seem to impart the idea they only like to talk to young sexy girls. They are bored with all other women. Remember, the 50 year old woman may be the Chairman of the Board, or C.E.O. of her company. Treat her with respect and interest. She has the money to buy.

Once when I had luncheon at a beautiful restaurant with a young salesman we were inter-rupted by a fashion show of beautiful models. He asked the first one: "Would you be so kind as to tell the models not to stop to talk at this table. We are holding a business meeting, and I do not want to miss a word my customer says." I bought the business machine I needed from him.

3. Ask Questions. My friend of the mind, Ben Franklin, says, "Put on the role of the humble inquirer." We all hate the canned sales talk that goes on and on, with no questions about our needs.

An example is the microwave oven. Women do not buy them for the machinery. They buy them because when they rush home from work, they want to get the family's dinner ready in a hurry. Quick cooking is what they purchase. We buy what the machine will do for us. The results.

So don't start with your sales talk. Begin with gentle, interested questions. "How will you be using it?" What do you need to accomplish?" "What is most important to you, size, safety, color? Tell me about your needs." Then show the woman buyer that your product or service will be the perfect solution for her problem. Tell her you want her to have it, that she deserves it.

4. Include her in the conversation. Ask her what she is going to use the car for. To haul horses? Then talk about horses. To deliver orders? Ask about her business. To run children around to their activities? Talk about safety. Don't go on and on about sports if she says she loves flowers and has a flower business. Talk about her business. Be interested in her life, her business, her family. So few men do this with women, you will be a stand out.

There is an old story of a young man who took a lovely girl out for a date. He spent most of the evening talking about himself. Finally, realizing he was monopolizing the conversation, he said, "Enough about me! I'll be quiet now, and give you a chance to talk about me for awhile."

5. Don't call her "honey, baby, dolly or sexy." Some women buyers will get mad and leave. Some will just seethe inwardly. These names are not funny, they are insulting. Ask her for her name. Give her yours. Call her by her name in a respectful way. Remember the way Elvis Presley called every woman he met Ma'am?" They loved it.

6. Get in step with her. If your Woman Buyer speaks rapidly, answer in the same fashion. If she speaks slowly, go at a quieter pace. Tune in on her. See her dream. Whatever she tells you, make notes. Be her buyer's assistant.

One of the greatest salesmen I ever met helped me to buy a gorgeous Pontiac Catalina. It was lime green and cream. So beautiful. So expensive. He asked many questions about my advertising business. He was interested. He invited me to sit down, got me a cold soft drink.

He explained that I deserved the very best car available. I had worked so hard. He wanted me to have a car that would look good with my blonde-red hair, and would not break down when I needed it. That certainly made sense to me!

He told me I would easily pay for this gorgeous

car, by setting new goals, raising my prices, selling more prestige accounts.

Then he capped his ideas with the thought that I should have the name of my company painted on the door. I did it all. He was right. My Catalina changed my image. I began hiring people in my advertising business. Opened a second office. We set our sights higher and grew. Those payments were not hard to make, because I loved that car.

One day when I was turning my scrumptious automobile around, two little boys stood on the sidewalk watching me. I called to them to stand still and not go into the driveway where I was turning.

One poked the other in the ribs and said, "Who is that?"

The other replied in a haughty tone, "Can't you see? **That lady is the Queen of the Bees!**"

Even the little children could see my new image. My car salesman was responsible for my business prospering, because he saw what I could do.

7. Get a "her side" attitude. Whenever possible sit on the same side of the desk. Put on the role of her helper. You are not there to fight with her, or to be a verbal adversary. She doesn't want to arm wrestle with you to get what she wants to buy.

Zig Ziglar tells the story of the best sales person in the pot and pan company he worked for as a young man. This sales lady would sit down on the davenport in the home of her prospect. She laid out her catalog of pots and pans in front of them. Then she said, "Tell me about all of those worn out, banged up pots in your kitchen that they expect you to work with."

After the customer itemized the old pans on hand, the saleswoman would shake her head and say, "No man would be expected to do good work with worn out tools like that."

"These pots and pans here in my catalog are what the big chefs use. The very best. The kind you deserve. Down at the factory those men have these good cooking tools stacked up to the ceiling! Now you just pick out what you need for your work. **I'm going to he'p you get them away from those men!**"

8. Use blarney, not baloney. Blarney is the varnished truth — it consists of caring and kindness. Baloney is an unvarnished lie. Calling an older woman "cute" is baloney. A woman knows a false compliment that you don't mean. It makes her mad.

Blarney is something else. It is fun. An older woman can be wise, intelligent, witty, elegant, charming. She may be a genius at her work, have a great memory. Appreciate her for what she is. Blarney is a glow on your words. It makes her smile.

9. Be a friend. The word "sell" comes from a Scandinavian root that literally means "to serve." The bible tells us that the greatest of us must be servant of all. The more we serve, the more value we have.

A salesperson who approaches the Woman Buyer with an interested, friendly, service attitude will be called again and again, and recommended to others. Women love to tell each other about good beauticians, caterers, all kinds of services. Many are the businesses built on these friendly referrals.

10. Ask her what color she likes. Remember, women are never color blind. Many men are. Color is much more important to a woman. A man may not care what color the car or truck is. In fact, sometimes he actually cannot see the difference. Not so with women.

A woman wears a car, a couch or wallpaper. She wants it to complement her personal coloring. She is particular about it. She understands that colors themselves are emotional. When she is mad, she sees red. Does a man shirk his duty? He is yellow. Is she sad? She feels blue. When she is in love, it is with a purple passion.

Women often say, "I have to get this room painted, I can't work here with this color." Don't argue with her. Help her to get what she wants. When you deal with a woman buyer, she wants it all. Service, prompt delivery, good price, and she wants it in a sharp becoming color.

11. Recognize her intelligence. Don't be like a salesman who called on me to sell my company a computer. Since I am the President of four corporations, I make these decisions.

He began by asking me when the "Boss" would be there. Then he set up a flip chart on my desk and began reading the 3 word pages to me. I gently told him that I am a speed reader. Then I explained that I wanted to buy the machine to solve some problems and asked if we could discuss the solutions.

"No use in doing that, baby. Your husband is not here to authorize the deal."

My smile froze. I gritted my teeth, got up, and suggested he call some other time. Then I immediately dialed his competitor.

The competitor began by asking me to tell them all about the things I would like the machine to do for my business. **They sold me the solutions to my problems. I bought from them.**

11. Remember, all women are not the same. Every woman knows in her heart of hearts that she is unique. A famous perfume, "Windsong," became world famous with a series of ads picturing a handsome young man in a dreamy mood. The copy ran: "Our perfume smells different on every woman, because every woman is unique. Wear Windsong and he won't be able to get you out of his mind."

Unique Customer Qualifier

A California Cadillac saleswoman named Sue said she likes to work with women. She tells them, "I'll work hard for you."

She gets over on their side. To qualify the woman buyer, Sue pops the hood of a car. If the woman leans forward and ask questions about the motor, Sue knows her woman buyer is mechanical. She then talks motors and technical information.

But if the woman buyer says, "I don't understand what makes the car work! I just want it to go!" then Sue has a different technique. She tells her Woman Buyer that she will personally go with her to the service department each time she brings the car back in for service. Then she shows her a beautiful key holder and a gold key. Sue says, "When you buy your car from me, we'll keep it purring. The only thing you will need is the key. And just to be sure you don't ever run out of keys, I am going to give you 4 extra ones, just like this, in holders to match this gorgeous upholstery. **You and I know the greatest happiness on earth is having the car key when you need it.**"

Then, after Sue writes up the order just the way her Woman Buyer wants it, she asks her who she knows who needs her help.

Sue, the Cadillac salesperson, aims where the puck is going.

12. Women are smell conscious. They buy 90% of mens toiletries. If your product has a smell, be sure to let her sniff it.

Women Buyers like to feel and hold things. A famous cosmetic firm instructs their salespeople to hand the product to the customer. They find 50% of those who hold the item will buy it.

Women are ear conscious. Napoleon Bonapart said, "Men make love with their eyes. Women with their ears." Women want to look beautiful so that men will be attracted to them. But they are attracted to men who are charming, articulate, witty and interested. Being fun is the #1 virtue women list as desirable in a mate. A woman likes a man who talks to her.

Stanford University reports: "Women have better hearing, mentally visualize better, are more conscious of color as it relates to emotion."

Practice These Magic Words

What is your dream? Would you tell me about it? How will you use it? What is most important to you? May I show you something new? Would you help me? Please hold this for a moment. Tell me if you like this. What if? How do you see it? What do you think? Would you be so kind as to recommend me to your friends? Who do you know that I could serve today?

When the Woman Buyer answers, try these responses:

Me too. That is my favorite. Wonderful choice. I admire women like you who... Great taste. You deserve it. We are proud to serve you.

Thank you, I appreciate... Feel the weight, solid. Quality. You are MY KIND of customer. I want you to have it. Count on me. I'll take care of it. I'll take care of all the details. It was such a pleasure. I enjoyed working with you. Let's set another appointment for next week.

As I tell audiences around the world, the new Woman Buyer has lots of money. She looks upon herself as brave. She likes to be appreciated for her unique talents and abilities. She wants a good buy, but in the color she prefers. She wants you to be her friend, mentor and advisor. She is worth the effort, because she will go out of her way to recommend you to her friends.

Bruce Barton, the great advertising genius, of Barton, Batten, Durstin and Osborn, said he based every ad he ever wrote on the **second** verse of "Mary had a little lamb.

"Why does the lamb love Mary so?"
The eager children cry.
"Mary loves the lamb, you know."
The teacher did reply.

Then Mr. Barton said, **"It is time we quit shearing these sheep and started loving them a little bit."**